WISCONSIN

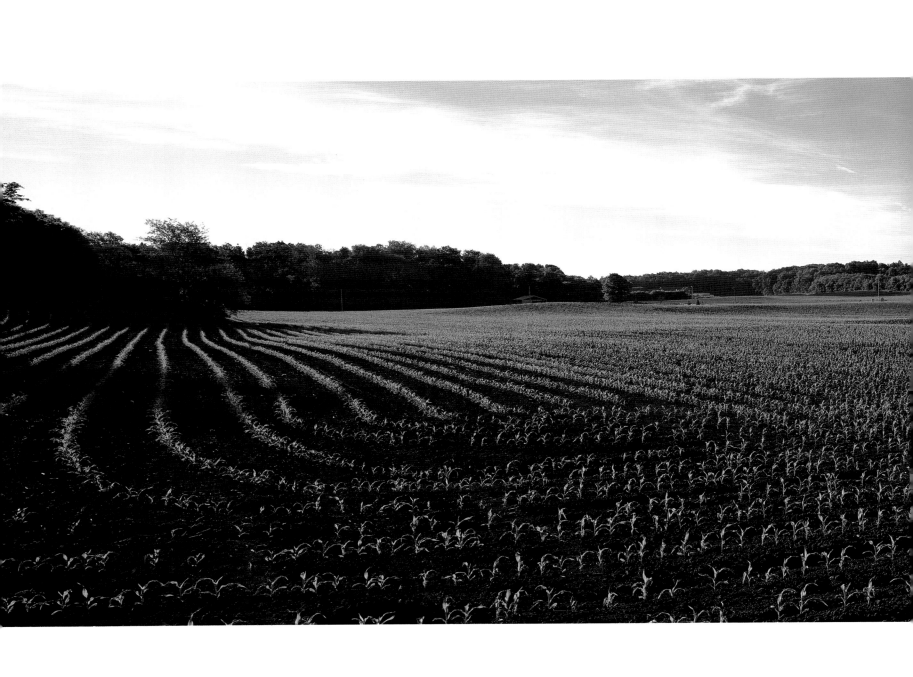

WISCONSIN

photography by
ZANE WILLIAMS

essays by
MARK LEFEBVRE

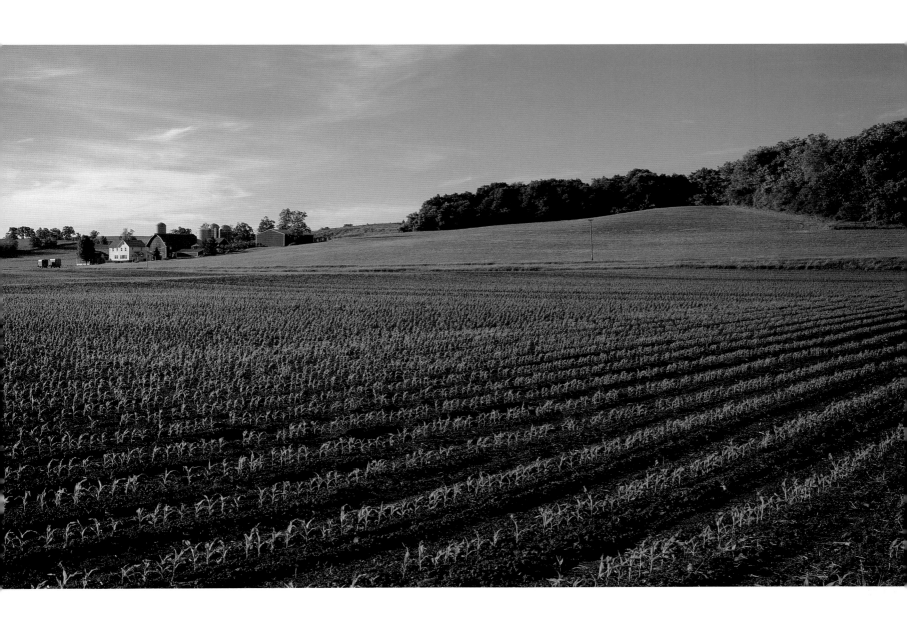

GRAPHIC ARTS CENTER PUBLISHING®

Revised Edition with Preface by Mark Lefebvre
International Standard Book Number 1-55868-404-2
Library of Congress Catalog Number 97-80274
Photographs and captions © MCMXCVIII by Zane Williams
Essays and Preface © MCMXCVIII by Mark Lefebvre
Published by Graphic Arts Center Publishing Company
P.O. Box 10306, Portland, Oregon 97296-0306
503/226-2402; www.gacpc.com
The quotations from August Derleth, Robert E. Gard, and
Owen J. Gromme are used with the permission of their
respective estates. The quotation from George Vukelich
is used with the author's permission.
President • Charles M. Hopkins
Editor-in-Chief • Douglas A. Pfeiffer
Managing Editor • Jean Andrews
Production Manager • Richard L. Owsiany
Cartographer • Ortelius Design
Book Manufacturing • Lincoln & Allen Co.
Printed in Hong Kong
Third Printing, Revised Edition

Title page: Spring corn, Dane County

WISCONSIN

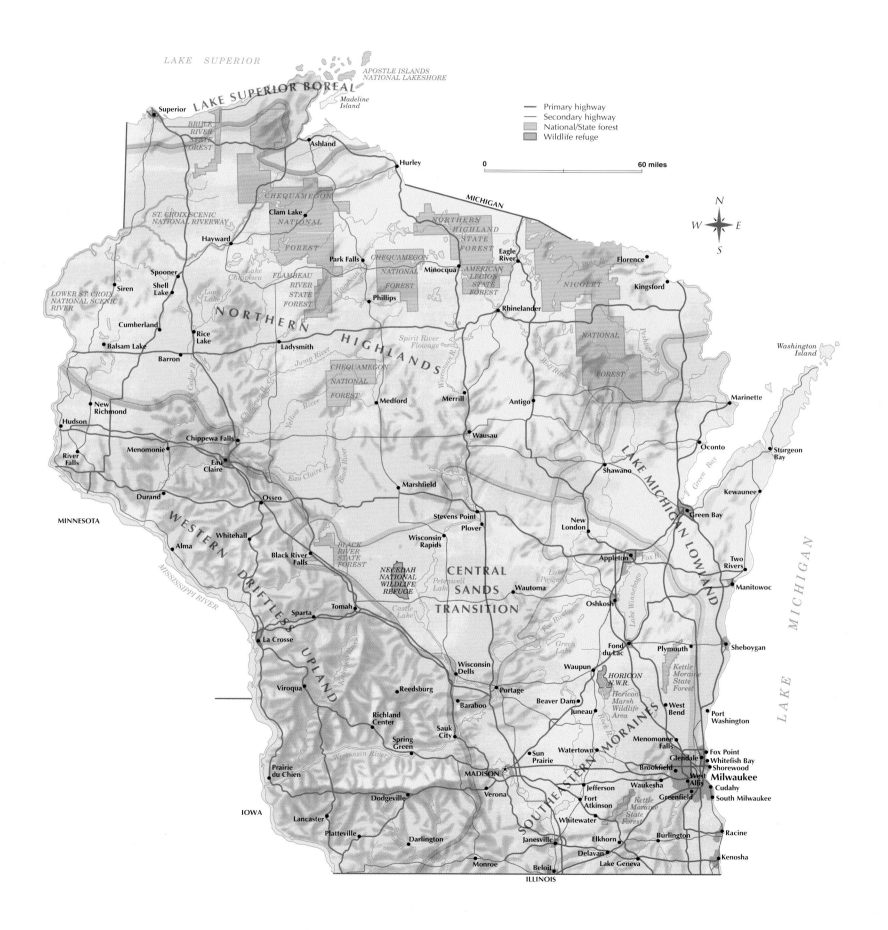

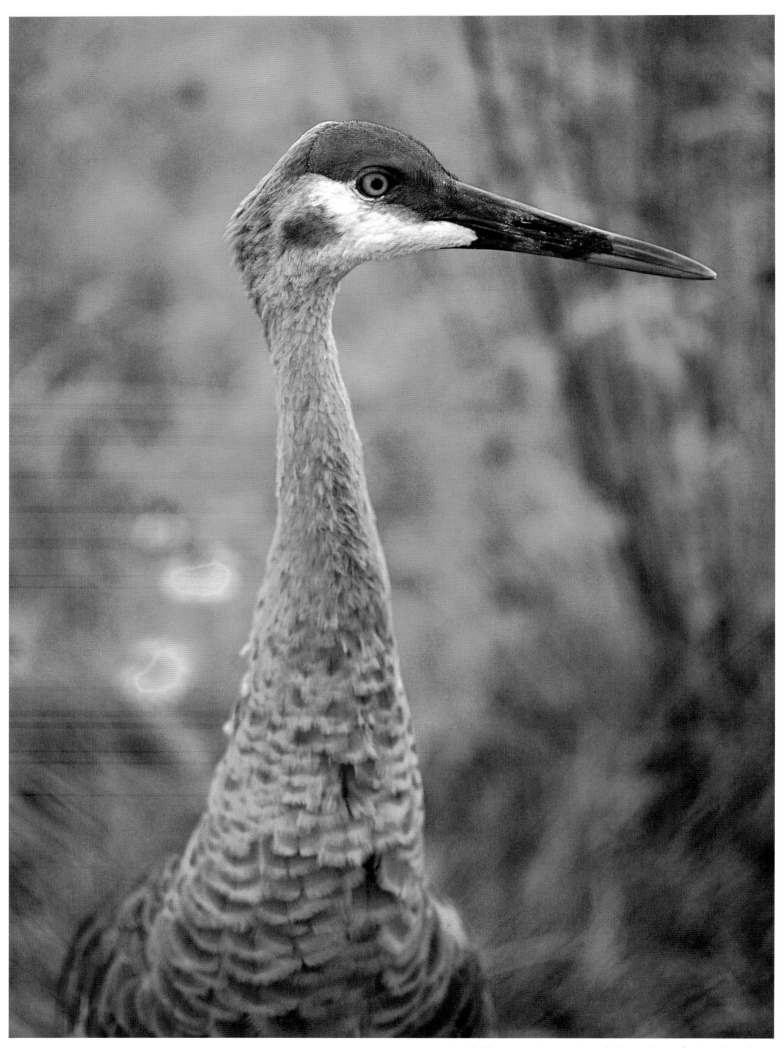

Sandhill crane, International Crane Foundation, Baraboo

PREFACE

REFLECTIONS ON WISCONSIN. As I reflect on the history of Wisconsin, I reflect on my personal history growing up on the banks of the Fox River at DePere, *Rapides des Peres,* "Rapids of the Fathers." The parish of my boyhood was founded in 1671 by one of these fathers, Claude Allouez. I spent my summer nights watching the old men put down their nets for smelt and I thought of the Potawatami before them. I hiked out of town to "the Ledge," the Niagara Escarpment, and explored the caves bearing their ancient petroglyphs. Like those before me, I was an explorer.

For someone coming of age in Wisconsin, my childhood was not unique. All of us would sit in our classrooms listening to the Wisconsin School of the Air. Robert E. Gard told stories about mythical creatures, like the hodag, who roamed the north. He also told us compelling stories of the settlers who came to Wisconsin to create homeplaces. These settlers were our ancestors. He was telling us the *living* history of Wisconsin.

Our forebears made Wisconsin a state on May 29, 1848. We were the thirtieth state to enter the Union. Governor Henry Dodge chose Belmont as the site of the first capital, but a shrewder politician, James Duane Doty, sparked a spirited contest during which Madison was selected as the permanent capital.

It has been said that after the frontier has been settled, perhaps after statehood is achieved, a new frontier emerges in the imaginations of the people who live there. Nowhere does the imagination flourish more than in Wisconsin. Here is where the "Wisconsin Idea" was born. It grew out of a willingness to experiment in meeting the changing needs of the people and the state. It brought together the state and the University of Wisconsin.

Governor Robert M. La Follette and President Charles Van Hise were the popularizers of the Idea making the boundaries of the University, the boundaries of the state and seeking to explore all ideas in a progressive spirit.

If you live in Wisconsin, you become part of its evolving history. You also develop a relationship with the land because the natural world here is one of wonder. When Zane Williams came to me to discuss the concept for this book, we both realized that the story of Wisconsin is rooted in an understanding of the land, the history of the state, and its culture—the way we live.

I was personally blessed in having three extraordinary mentors: Robert E. Gard, August Derleth, and Owen J. Gromme. Gard and Derleth as writers and Gromme as a visual artist, devoted their lives to the exploration of Wisconsin, the people and the natural environment. Gard and Derleth were regionalists in every sense of the word. They believed that one's roots went deepest when one possessed a real sense of place. They celebrated the land and the uniqueness of those who lived on it. Gard, especially, cherished the dignity and possibilities of day-to-day life in Wisconsin. Gromme, an explorer from boyhood, walked the marshes, woods, and thickets of his native state, distilling lessons on canvas for all of us. The words of these men echo throughout this book.

As Wisconsin enters the twenty-first century, we reflect on the past, on the Millennium, on our new century. Each of us is an explorer. In my own dream, I am accompanying the first explorer to Wisconsin, Jean Nicolet, as he experiences landfall at Red Banks in 1634. Gard, Derleth, and Gromme are with us, and we are all eager to chronicle and capture what we see. It is a place like no other.

I wish you well as you journey through *Wisconsin.*

MARK LEFEBVRE

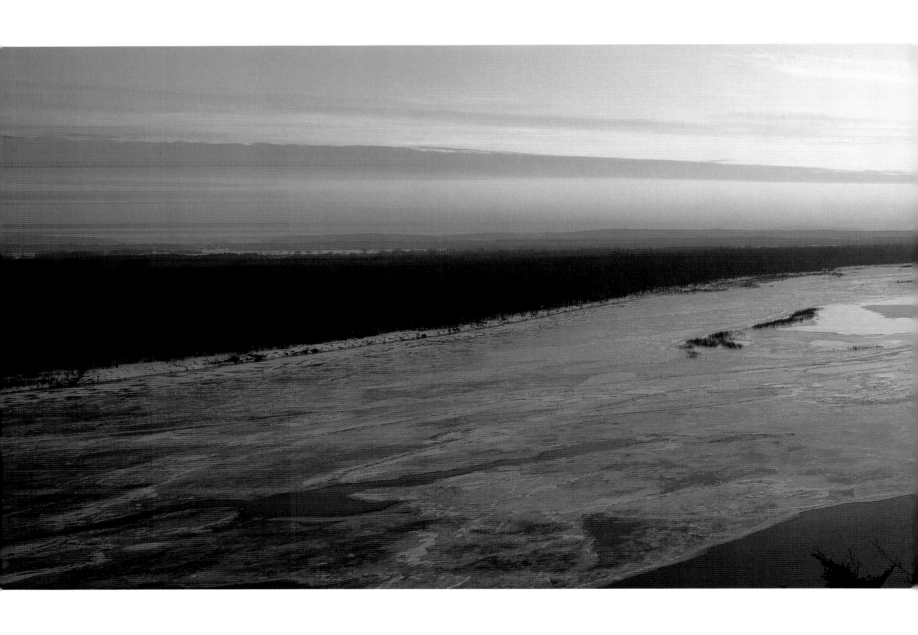

*I remember looking out from Ferry Bluff
across the winter landscape, across the
sweep of the Wisconsin River, and thinking
of those who looked out here before me.*

AUGUST DERLETH

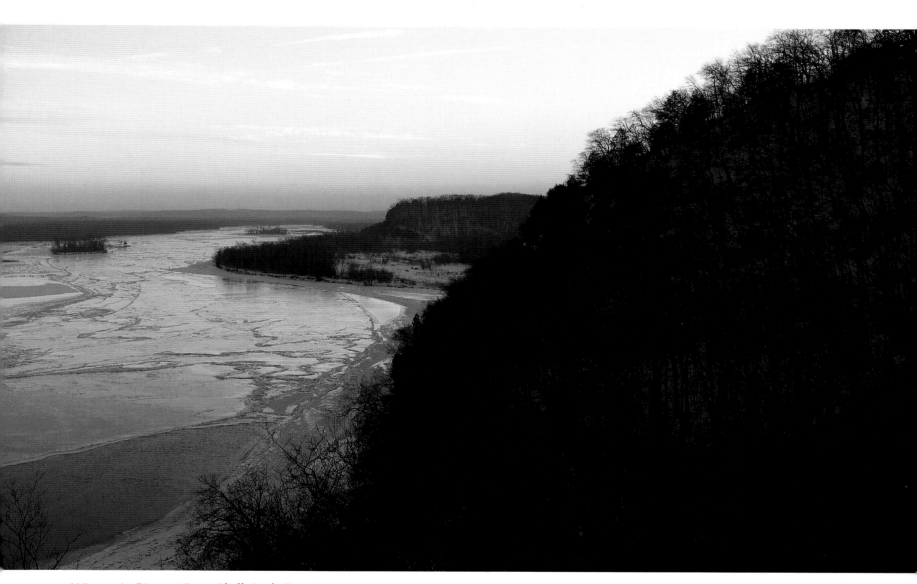

Wisconsin River at Ferry Bluff, Sauk County

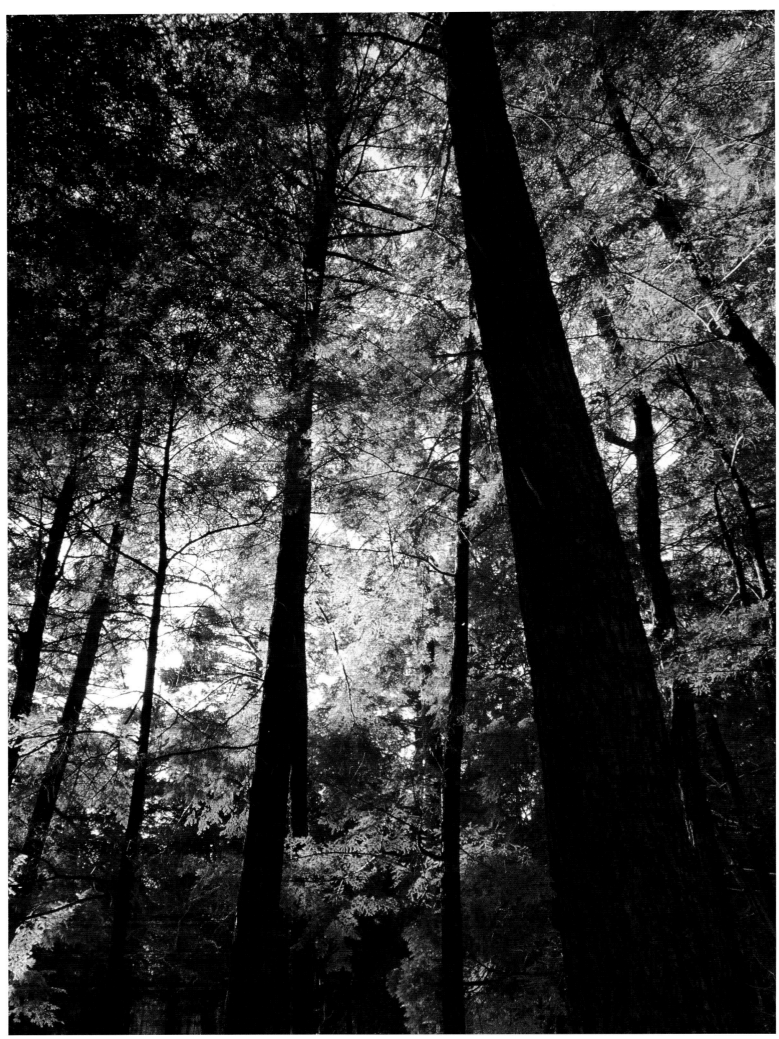

Giant White Pine Grove, Northern Highland Region

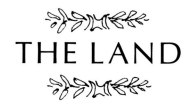

THE LAND

GEOGRAPHICAL ORIGINS OF THE LAND. Much of the land we know today as Wisconsin began in flame, molten rock, and enormous clouds of steam. There were mountains of granite and other rocks born of fire, and there was a great sea. Cataclysmic earth movements shook the land to its very core. Great volcanos spewed forth molten rock, and the very earth folded over on itself.

All this happened one and a half billion years ago, long before there was life on the earth. But the evidence is clear to geologists, who can paint pictures from the outlines left behind in stone.

Millions of years of erosion flattened Wisconsin's northern mountains, only to have the earth erupt repeatedly. Eventually, around five hundred million years ago, the first life appeared in Wisconsin's great seas—crabs, shellfish, trilobites, seaweed. They were soon (in geologic terms) joined by other sea creatures, including sharks and fierce-looking bony fish.

There is no record of dinosaurs in Wisconsin, but the age of mammals that followed was a very active period. Great mastodons and hairy mammoths roamed the land, as did saber-toothed tigers, horned bison, five-hundred-pound beavers, deer, and caribou. The skeleton of an eight-ton mastodon stands today in the geology museum of the University of Wisconsin-Madison.

These giant creatures were slowly driven south as the climate grew colder and gigantic sheets of ice, a mile or more high and hundreds of miles wide, advanced into Wisconsin from Canada, beginning some two million years ago. Advancing relentlessly, the ice changed forever everything in its path. The weight of the ice flattened hills, ground rocks into clay and mud, and pushed boulders and topsoil down from Canada into the middle of Wisconsin. The glaciers advanced and retreated as many as

twenty times during the last Ice Age, and about eleven thousand years ago dug the Great Lakes and left thousands of smaller lakes, streams, and rivers behind, as well.

The Kettle Moraine country of southeastern Wisconsin yields evidence of the work of glaciers. Mounds of glacial drift are interspersed with depressions, or "kettles," formed by melting of subterranean ice blocks. When glaciers changed the Wisconsin River's course, they formed the gorges in the Wisconsin Dells.

THE DRIFTLESS AREA. However, glaciers did not cover all of Wisconsin. Missed were about fifteen thousand square miles, most of them in southwestern Wisconsin, when the tongue of the glacier became forked. It separated near Stevens Point, one fork crossing the Mississippi River near Alma, the other following a line including the Wisconsin Dells and Baraboo.

The unglaciated or "driftless" area has quite different geological features from those found to the north. Rivers and streams run through deep gorges, ancient weathered rocks, and much more rugged and varied terrain. Mesas, escarpments, and chimney rocks—formed by uneven weathering of rock—dot the area.

Devil's Lake, near Baraboo, is perhaps the most spectacular of the remaining evidence of the driftless area. Here are towering quartzite bluffs, created by ancient earth upheavals that took place long before the glaciers. Here also is a deep, clear lake, formed when the glaciers changed the course of the Wisconsin River and dammed up both ends of the gorge. Today, Devil's Lake is the most popular state park in Wisconsin.

Visitors today can see vestiges of the Ice Age by touring segments of the Ice Age National Scenic Trail, a thousand-mile course that runs from the Door Peninsula (Wisconsin's "thumb," extending into Lake Michigan) through the Kettle Moraine, across the center of the state, and northwest to the St. Croix River.

The geological history of Wisconsin has almost dictated the history of its people. The glaciers left behind more than seven thousand lakes, fifty-six thousand square miles of inland water (not counting the Great Lakes), and provided a superb natural system of inland waterways that have encouraged commerce and trade. The great ice sheets not only brought mineral-rich soil down from the north, but they also ground rocks into a fine powder, thus making them available for the growth of great forests and fertile fields. Left behind were rich deposits of metals—copper, iron, lead, zinc. Extensive layers of limestone provided ideal building blocks. Fish and wildlife were abundant, from the times of the earliest human inhabitants until today. It is no wonder that human life has flourished in this land, almost from the very beginning.

FLORA AND FAUNA. Although Wisconsin has the reputation of being a northwoods state, it is actually only partly so. In the north, it is certainly part of the boreal forests that stretch all the way to the tundra. In the south, however, Wisconsin is prairie country, sharing more flora with Iowa and Kansas than with Michigan's Upper Peninsula and Canada. The large middle section of Wisconsin is a land where needleleaf white pine and broadleaf sugar maples grow side by side. This transitional forest offers not only a wide variety of plants, but a richness of animal life, as well.

When Europeans arrived in Wisconsin, the southern prairie lands featured savannas with oak groves, glacial lakes, marshes, and sedge meadows. North of the prairies were vast forests of oak, ash, basswood, cherry, maple, tamarack, hickory, walnut, elm, hemlock, yellow birch, beech, and pine. In the far north were thick forests of fir, spruce, pine, hemlock, and cedar.

The rich black prairie soil attracted farmers and homesteaders, while the northern forests brought loggers. Within a single century, ending about 1930, most old-growth red and eastern white pines in Wisconsin had been depleted. In the south, wheat was king on the prairies for a while; however, eventually the land was found to be more hospitable to dairy farming, which remains the leading agribusiness in the state today.

Running generally in a northwest to southeast direction, a tension zone demarcates Wisconsin's natural vegetation. Boreal forests dominate north of the zone, while prairie elements dominate the south. In the broad middle band, plants of both regions freely mix. Still, vacationers driving north can easily notice the change in scenery as they move through the tension zone.

Hardwood species common to the eastern United States—oak, maple, beech, hickory, basswood, ash—dominate the forests in the southwest. Elms were once very prominent, but most have now fallen to Dutch Elm disease. On prairie remnants, clusters of oak trees, called oak openings, still thrive. Oaks were the only trees tough enough to survive the periodic prairie fires.

The north features conifers—including pine, spruce, hemlock, fir, cedar, and tamarack—usually mixed with hardwoods. With its diverse climate and topography, Wisconsin supports a great assortment of shrubs and wildflowers, including most common forest and meadow species found in the eastern United States.

Wisconsin bird life also offers a wide variety. Besides the rich divergence of waterfowl that migrate along the Mississippi Flyway and through Wisconsin, there are hundreds of species of songbirds, raptors, and other birds. Ample opportunities also exist for watching these birds. The International Crane Foundation, the Horicon National Wildlife Refuge, the Schlitz Audubon Center, and the numerous state-sponsored wildlife areas are valuable resources for Wisconsin's citizens and visitors.

The animal life in the state is also varied and impressive. Yes, badgers are there, but so are black bears, pumas, and a host of smaller animals of field and forest—raccoons, weasels, beavers, muskrats, squirrels, mink, gophers, hares, rabbits, and more. The white-tailed deer population is large, bringing a rich harvest for hunters every autumn. Fishing is even more popular. Hundreds of streams offer brown, brook, and rainbow trout, while the lakes hold out rich catches of muskellunge, pike, walleye, and bass.

LAND OF WATER. Sculpted by glaciers, Wisconsin's land is still dominated by water; its climate is greatly affected by water; its history has been shaped by water; and water continues to be a determining influence in nearly every aspect of life today—from agriculture to industry to tourism.

Wisconsin lies in the middle of the Upper Great Lakes, the world's largest concentration of fresh water. Lakes Superior, Huron, and Michigan alone contain more than seventy-seven thousand square surface miles of water. Wisconsin has more than fourteen thousand inland lakes, nine thousand of which are larger than twenty acres. In addition, the great Mississippi River forms the state's western border with Minnesota and Iowa, connecting the area to the ports of St. Louis, Memphis, and New Orleans.

Thousands of years before Europeans introduced railroads and highways to this area, river routes provided the swiftest and easiest transportation routes for the Native peoples. The Chippewa, Fox, Sioux, Winnebago, Sauk, Ottawa, and others built their villages along the lakes and rivers. Water provided opportunity to harvest fish, assured irrigation for crops, and served as an access point for trading missions to other regions. Water was the chief avenue of commerce for centuries. The extensive water network enabled the tribes to trade with each other since before the age of the Egyptian Pharaohs. When the French explorers discovered the region's wealth of fur-bearing animals—chiefly beaver—in the seventeenth century, water routes provided entry to a productive fur trade with the Native peoples, ushering in the age of the voyageurs. Pelts, harvested and cured by the Natives, were traded to the French, then later to the British, before moving across the Great Lakes and the St. Lawrence to eastern ports.

By the 1830s, just as the fur trade was diminishing, lakes and rivers floated millions of tons of logs from Wisconsin's north woods to ready markets to the south, east, and west, supplying the growing needs of the burgeoning new nation.

Today, the St. Lawrence Seaway transports materials from the Superior/Duluth harbor to the Atlantic—more than twenty-three hundred miles—where they are then disbursed to the rest of the world. Ships carrying lumber, iron ore, and wheat ply the route from Duluth to Sault Ste. Marie, into Lake Huron, around Detroit, and straight on to the East Coast. Giant ore carriers supply the steel

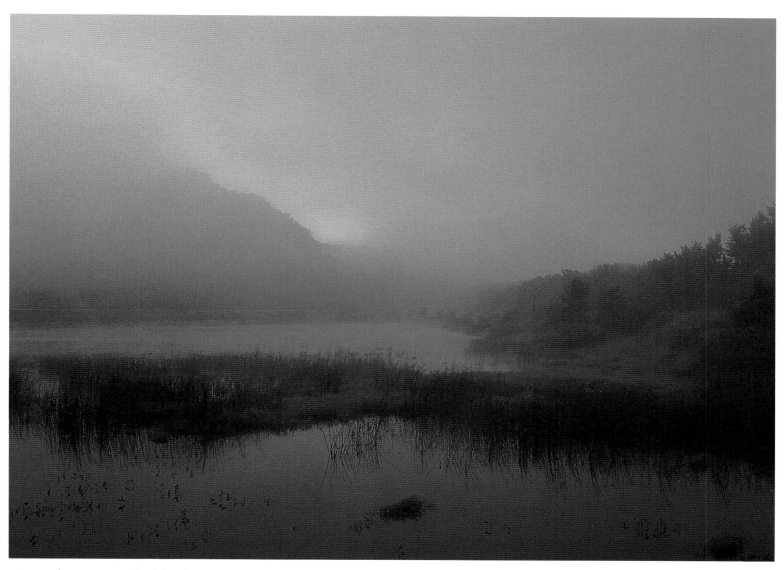

History has no record of the beginnings of the Mississippi River. Relatively unaffected by geologic change through history, its upper reaches move in meandering patterns along the state's western boundary, hemmed in by high bluffs that keep its limits constricted.

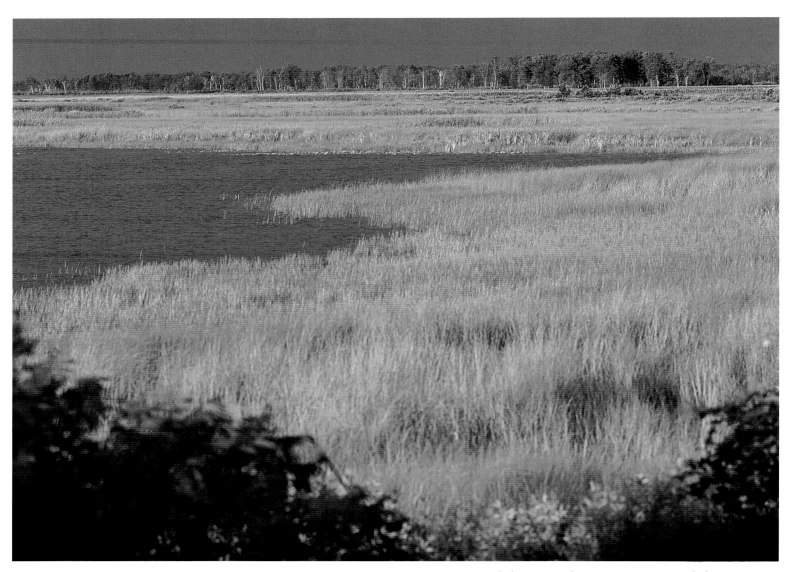

Representative of the presettlement vegetation of the extensive northwestern Wisconsin barrens area, Crex Sand Prairie in Burnett County occupies 26,000 acres of extensive sand plain that was once glacial Lake Grantsburg. Prior to white settlement in the mid-1800s, the Fox, Dakota, and Chippewa used Crex extensively. Today, the area is home to sharptail grouse, trumpeter swans, sandhill cranes, ospreys, eagles, cormorants, herons, mink, deer, and bear.

mills of Gary, Indiana, moving from Lake Huron's shores, through the Straits of Mackinac, and on down the Lake Michigan coast. Though the great water network is no longer the only major means of commercial transport, it remains a crucial one, even today.

The tremendous bounty of fish in the waters of Wisconsin has sustained human development since the very beginning. Native Americans, fishing with nets and spears, harvested enough white-fish, trout, and sturgeon to assure their winter food supply, even when bad-weather years diminished agricultural crops. Voyageurs depended on fresh fish for daily sustenance, and European settlers of the nineteenth century harvested or bought fish to supplement their food supplies. Even today, many families in rural Wisconsin depend on fish to supplement weekly diets.

Abundant water has always been critical to agriculture, as well. Large expanses of water stimulate rainfall for agricultural production, and allow ready irrigation of crops during infrequent dry periods. The climate-moderating influence of the Great Lakes even permits the growing of fruit varieties in northern latitudes where they could not ordinarily survive.

Still, most people today treasure Wisconsin's water for the recreation it provides. Big-time salmon fishing on Lake Michigan, pursuing the wily muskie on a northern lake, casting for brook trout in a fast-moving stream, or trolling for bass on a lazy afternoon—all bring fishing enthusiasts to the Badger State. A first-class state park system offers plenty of swimming, sailing, canoeing, and scuba diving. The sparkling waters, deep woods, and moderate temperatures combine to make Wisconsin the most popular summer tourist destination in the entire Midwest.

MARSHES, WETLANDS. Few natural areas of Wisconsin are treasured more highly than its wetlands and marshes. These are shallow basins scooped out by the last of the glaciers and covered with water for all or most of the year.

Wisconsin is home to extensive wetland areas, including the popular Horicon Marsh, a thirty-thousand-acre wildlife sanctuary, in the south-central part of the state. These areas not only provide for a rich diversity of flora and fauna, but also serve as a natural purifier of groundwater.

Wisconsin's marshes draw thousands of bird watchers, especially during bird migrations. At Horicon, nearly a quarter of a million Canada Geese gather every spring and fall. In the spring, they stop over on their way to nesting grounds at Hudson Bay; in the fall, as they travel south to the great refuges at Horseshoe Bend or Union County, where the Ohio and Mississippi rivers join.

The complex ecology of the marsh supports a tremendous variety of plant and animal life, all to the delight of visitors from early spring to late autumn. Here, visitors watch a muskrat build its jackstraw house from cattail stalks or observe red-winged blackbirds stake out their nesting territory in spring. They watch in fascination as an American bittern, exposing its vertically striped breast, cleverly disguises itself as some of the marsh reeds in which it hides. Careful observers can watch mink, turtles, frogs, fish, and an amazing variety of ducks and other waterfowl, both at migration time and through the warm-weather months.

The marshes served for thousands of years as an essential source of food and clothing for the Native American peoples.

Beginning with the coming of European settlers in the 1830s, many of the marshes were drained for farmland or were otherwise destroyed. Hunting and trapping brought some animal species nearly to extinction. Now, Wisconsin citizens are gaining a new respect for wetlands, not only as a preserver of natural diversity, but also as a guardian of precious groundwater.

WATERFALLS. In a state lacking mountains of any size, large waterfalls would hardly be expected. Still, Wisconsin, with more than three thousand miles of streams and rivers and a variety of rock formations, offers falls of great diversity and unusual beauty.

Most falls lie along the south shore of Lake Superior, although some are in Florence and Marinette counties and along the wild Wolf River, where rafting and whitewater canoeing are popular activities. Many of the most beautiful are in state parks, where they are appreciated by all.

Brownstone Falls, in Copper Falls State Park, Ashland County, sends water thirty feet over a black lava ledge, in a scene of rugged beauty. It is one of the state's most spectacular falls.

Sandstone and shale ledges form the basis of Bad River Falls, also in Ashland County, on the Bad River Indian Reservation.

Big Manitou Falls, in Douglas County, along the Black River, is the highest in Wisconsin, and—at 165 feet—one of the tallest falls east of the Mississippi River. It is located in Pattison State Park, which also offers some of the best trout fishing in the state.

Saxon Falls, in Iron County, hurls water from the Montreal River seventy feet between walls of massive, solid rock. Saxon Falls is not located in a park or other easily accessible area, but it—and others—can be found, with diligence and time. Some people have actually made a hobby of discovering Wisconsin's hidden waterfalls. Each discovery is that much sweeter for the effort.

RIVERS. The state is divided into three major watersheds. In the north, water drains into Lake Superior, and in the southeast, into Lake Michigan. Both eventually drain into the Atlantic through the St. Lawrence. In the southwest, the largest watershed drains into the Mississippi and goes on to the Gulf of Mexico. Major tributaries to the Mississippi include the St. Croix, Chippewa, Black, and Wisconsin rivers. The Rock River detours through Illinois on its way to the Mississippi River. Flowing north and east to the St. Lawrence are the Fox-Wolf-Lake-Winnebago system, the Menominee, Manitowoc, Sheboygan, and Milwaukee rivers. In the north, the Brule, Bad, and Montreal flow into Lake Superior.

The Mississippi is obviously the largest river touching the state of Wisconsin—and the first natural feature foreign visitors ask to see. The Wisconsin River, however, is more commonly heralded in the state—in myth, legend, and literature. While many other states share the Mississippi, the Wisconsin is truly Wisconsin's own. It has been called the hardest working river in America. Little known is that the state was named for the river, not vice versa. The Chippewas called it Wees-konsan, meaning "gathering of waters."

The Wisconsin begins as a small outlet stream from a lake on the border of Wisconsin and Michigan's Upper Peninsula—the Lac Vieux Desert. Less than ten feet wide and a foot deep at its source, it travels more than four hundred miles through Wisconsin, south through the center of the state, then turns west at Portage, and flows to the Mississippi. It drops 917 feet during its course, and is nearly a mile across as it joins the Mississippi at Prairie du Chien.

The first Europeans who saw the Wisconsin River were Father Jacques Marquette, five French-Canadian voyageurs, and fur trader Louis Jolliet, in 1673. From that time until the present, the Wisconsin has been the most important river in the state and the main conduit to the "great river" that runs to the sea.

SHOWCASING THE LAND. Wisconsin's state park system is one of the finest in the nation. Since the turn of the century, the state has wisely purchased and preserved some of its most beautiful natural areas, making them available to residents and visitors from all over the world. Today, more than seventy operating parks and other natural public areas encompass more than seventy thousand acres. In addition, four recreational forests comprise another forty-seven thousand acres.

Interstate Park, which straddles the St. Croix River on the border with Minnesota, was Wisconsin's first state park. It was created in cooperation with the Minnesota state government, which established its half on the other side of the river, in 1900. Since then, parks have been established in all parts of the state, so no resident today is more than an hour's drive from a state park.

Many parks have outstanding individual natural features, while others feature special themes. Heritage Hill State Park, in Green Bay, is a living museum depicting the early history of Green Bay and of the state. Visitors can see replicas of the state's oldest remaining home, a French missionary bark chapel, an authentic fur trader's cabin, and several military buildings.

Wisconsin's Door County peninsula—the "thumb" that extends into Lake Michigan—is the home of more state parks than any other county in the nation. Peninsula is the largest, at 3,763 acres; Newport, with thirteen acres of Lake Michigan and Europe Lake shoreline, is the newest. But people who like camping rough head for Rock Island State Park, off the peninsula's tip. The entire island is a rocky, forested, wilderness paradise, accessible only by boat. No motor vehicles are permitted.

Devil's Lake State Park, near Baraboo, was a resort long before it became a park. The tall, sheer quartzite bluffs surrounding the lake are a geologic wonder, so impressive that more than a hundred colleges and universities make geologic and geographic pilgrimages to Devil's Lake each year. It is Wisconsin's most popular state park, both because of its beauty and because it lies near a large population area. It is also the most popular rock climbing area between the East Coast and the Rocky Mountains.

Natural Bridge State Park, near Baraboo, features a natural sandstone bridge, created by water and surrounded by a beautiful wild area. Archaeologists say people lived here eleven thousand years ago, when the last glacier stopped only twelve miles away.

Rib Mountain State Park, just west of Wausau, is a popular area, summer and winter. At an elevation of 1,940 feet, no Colorado native would ever call this a real mountain, but it does offer some of the best downhill skiing in the state.

Tower Hill State Park, near Spring Green, includes a real shot tower where millions of pounds of lead were manufactured into ammunition in the early 1800s. Wildcat Mountain State Park, near Ontario, is designed for horseback riding. Bigfoot Beach State Park

has nineteen hundred feet of frontage on Lake Geneva, a prime resort area only a short drive from Chicago. Wyalusing State Park, high on bluffs overlooking the Mississippi River, offers breathtaking views year-round. Copper Falls State Park, way up north, provides some of the most wildly spectacular scenery of any park.

Most parks offer camping, along with fishing, boating, picnicking, and hiking. Many have nature education programs, including self-guided nature walks. Wisconsin is making efforts to increase winter use of the parks, too, with improved ski and snowmobile trails, winter camping areas, and special winter events. Two parks include downhill ski areas with lifts and tows.

Besides the parks, Wisconsin has a growing network of state trails, most built on abandoned railroad beds. They offer pleasant walking or bicycle riding in the warm months, and snowmobiling in the winter. The thirty-two-mile Elroy-Sparta State Trail features three old train tunnels, one of them three-fourths of a mile long.

CLIMATE. The popular impression is that Wisconsin is a land of snow and ice. In actual fact, the climate is quite temperate. As French explorer Radisson said, after his visit in 1656, "I can assure you I liked noe country, as I have that wherein we wintered [Wisconsin] . . . for because that the country was so pleasant, so beautiful and fruitfull that it grieved me to see that the world could not discover such inticing country to live in."

Though the state shares its northern latitude with Minnesota and the Dakotas, the winters here are milder and the summers cooler, all because of the moderating influence of the Great Lakes. Weather patterns, influenced by fronts that move generally east, produce a great variety of weather conditions.

Wisconsin's weather produces four distinct seasons. Summers are generally warm and pleasant, with sufficient rainfall for the growing of farm and garden crops. Because of this, Wisconsin has become the nation's leader in the growing of many vegetables for canning and freezing. Hundreds of thousands of tourists flock to the state's northern reaches every summer, to escape the heat of the cities. Even those in the state's populous southern areas relish a week or two "up north" when the warm days of July arrive.

Autumns are usually long and pleasant, with snow arriving in early November in the north and in late November in the south. The hardwood forests of the south produce a glorious display of color in October—reds and golds unfolding along the hillsides, interspersed with the greens and whites of pine and birch.

Winters can be long and cold, yet less severe than those in neighboring states in the same latitude. The Door Peninsula, which thrusts into Lake Michigan, has milder winters than those farther west. This area, for years a popular summer vacation destination, is now becoming a prime spot for winter vacationers, as well. Rather than dread the winter, Wisconsites—with the aid of space-age clothing materials—have learned to enjoy it.

Spring, eagerly awaited by most, is often unmercifully short, a brief interlude between winter snows and summer heat. It also is, weatherwise, totally unpredictable, a week of sunshine and temperatures in the 80s followed by a week of 50s and rain. Many gardens, planted early in May, must be replanted after Memorial Day. Still, Wisconsinites spend the last of winter looking for signs of spring, and relish its appearance as the door to summer fun.

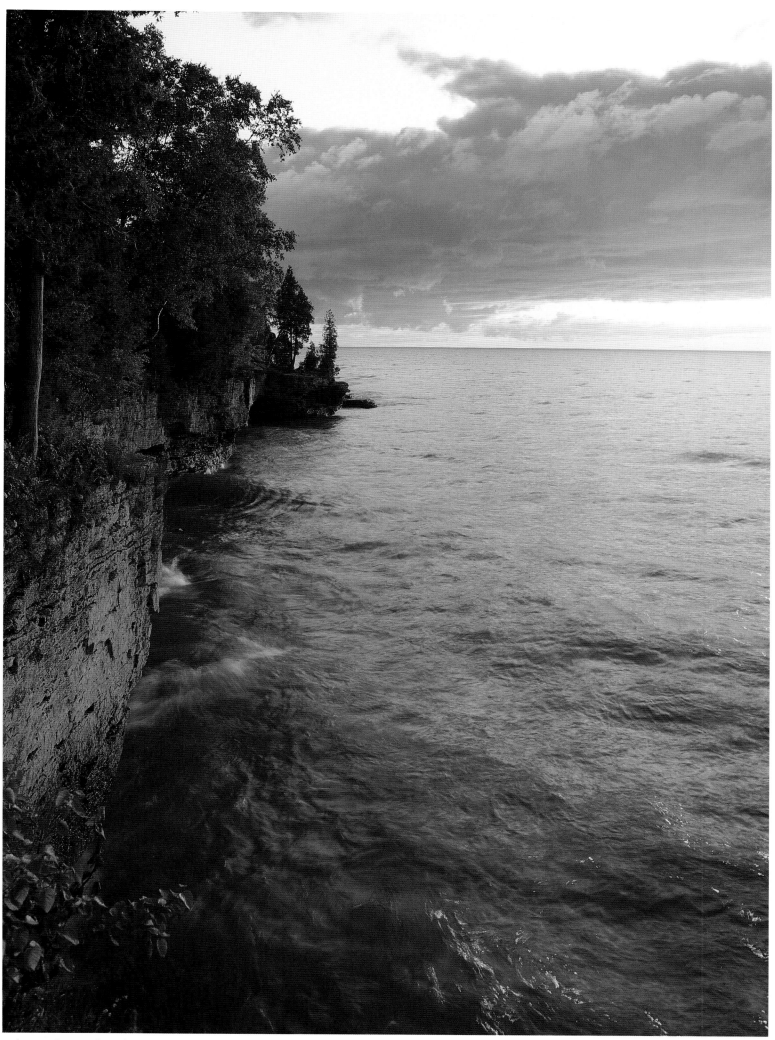

Lake Michigan shoreline at Cave Point, Door County

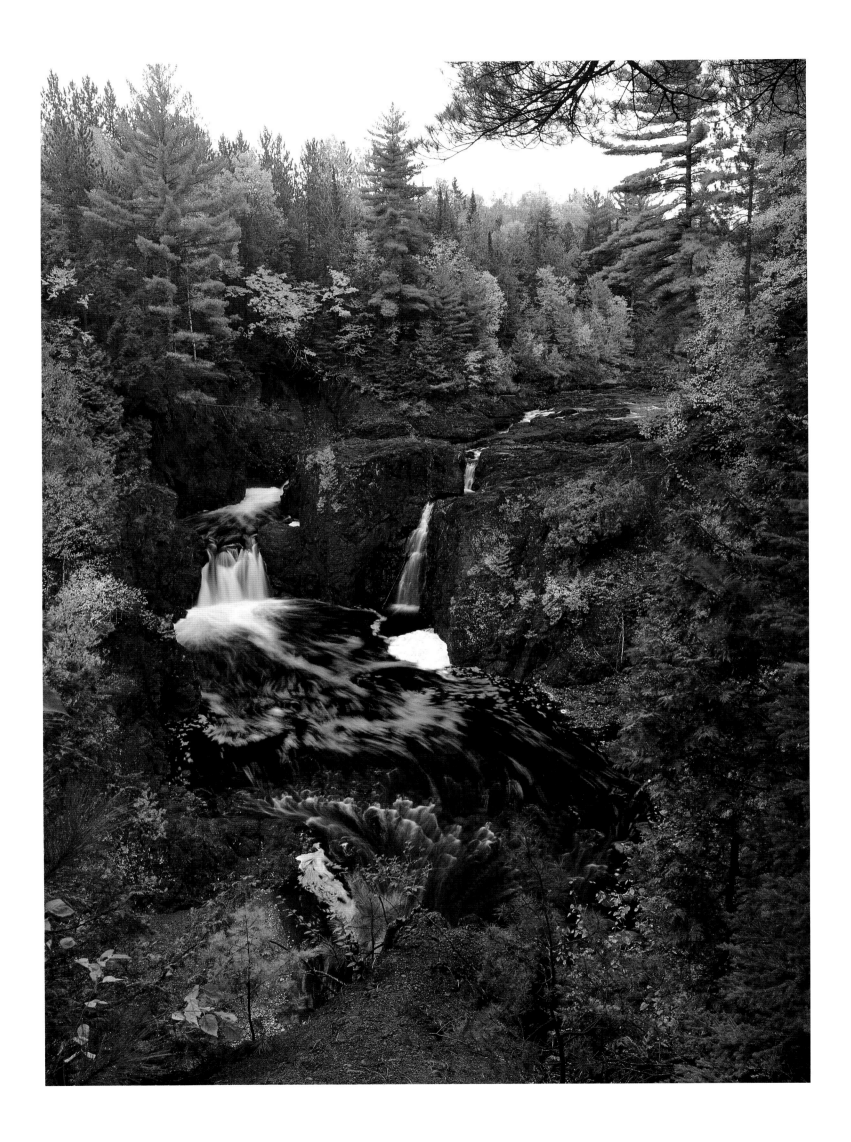

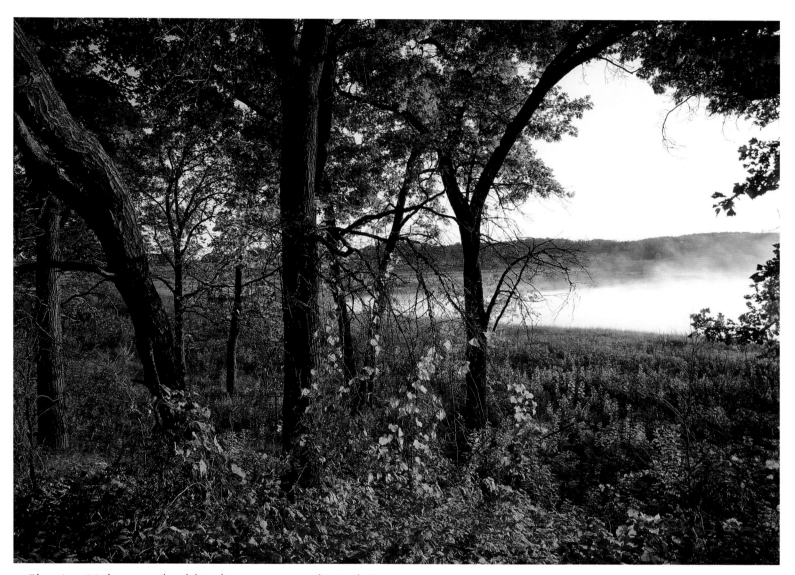

◄ Plunging 30 feet over hard basalt escarpments, the Bad River continues downstream from Copper Falls through sixty- to one hundred-foot gorges, forming one of the most spectacular parks in the state. Long before the glaciers, this area was part of the Penokean Range, home to some of the tallest mountains of all time.

▲ Lying within what is known as Wisconsin's "sand counties" is a landscape of wetlands, kettle lakes, dry-to-wet prairie, and oak savannas. John Muir County Park in Marquette County memorializes the site of Sierra Club founder John Muir's boyhood home, where his family settled in 1849 soon after Wisconsin statehood.

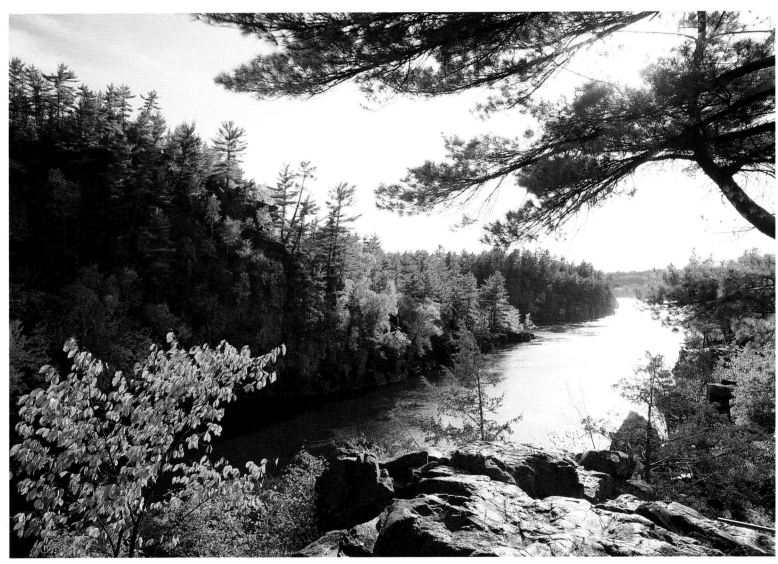

▲ Once a glacial drainway, the Dalles (French for "flagstone") of the St. Croix River, with its hundred-foot-deep gorge, Precambrian basalt walls, and water-formed potholes, became Wisconsin's first state park in 1900. Congress later designated it "wild and scenic."
► Overlooking the flat plain of Glacial Lake Wisconsin, Roche A Cri butte quickly rises three hundred feet, perhaps the steepest hill in the state. Both natives and pioneers watched for this landmark.

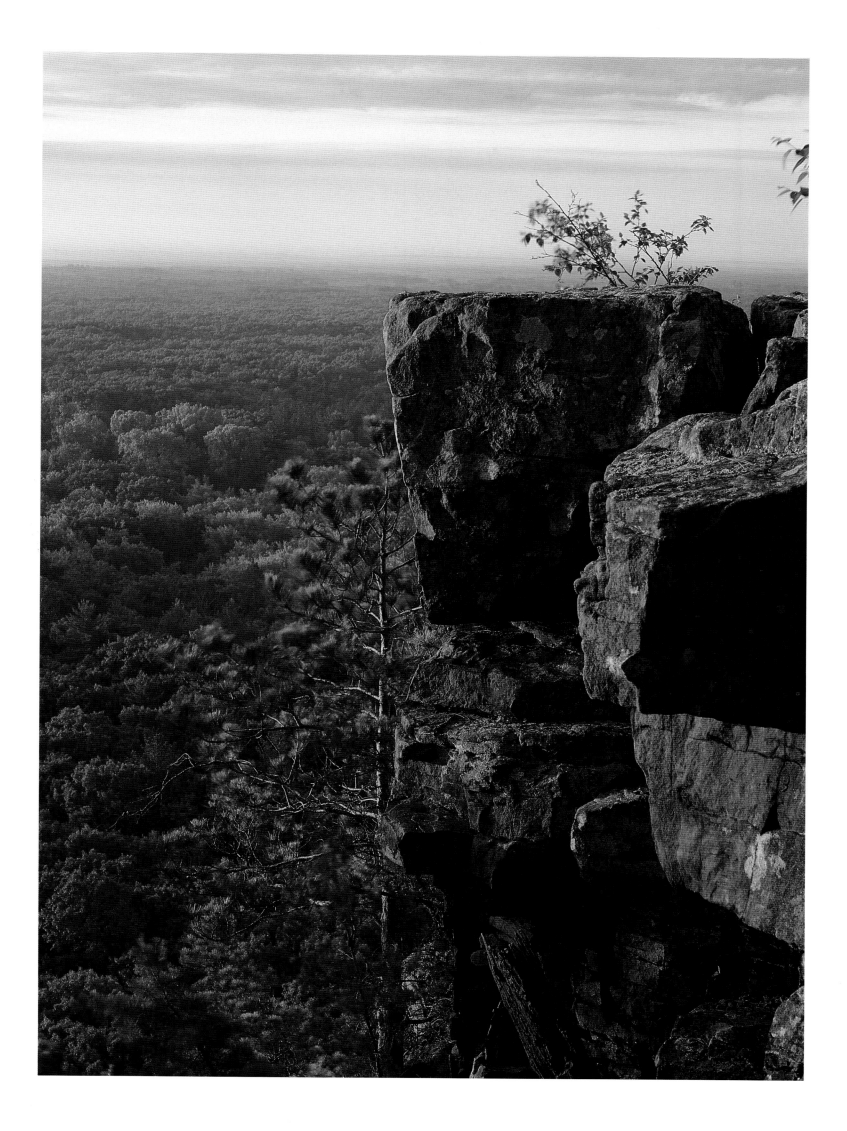

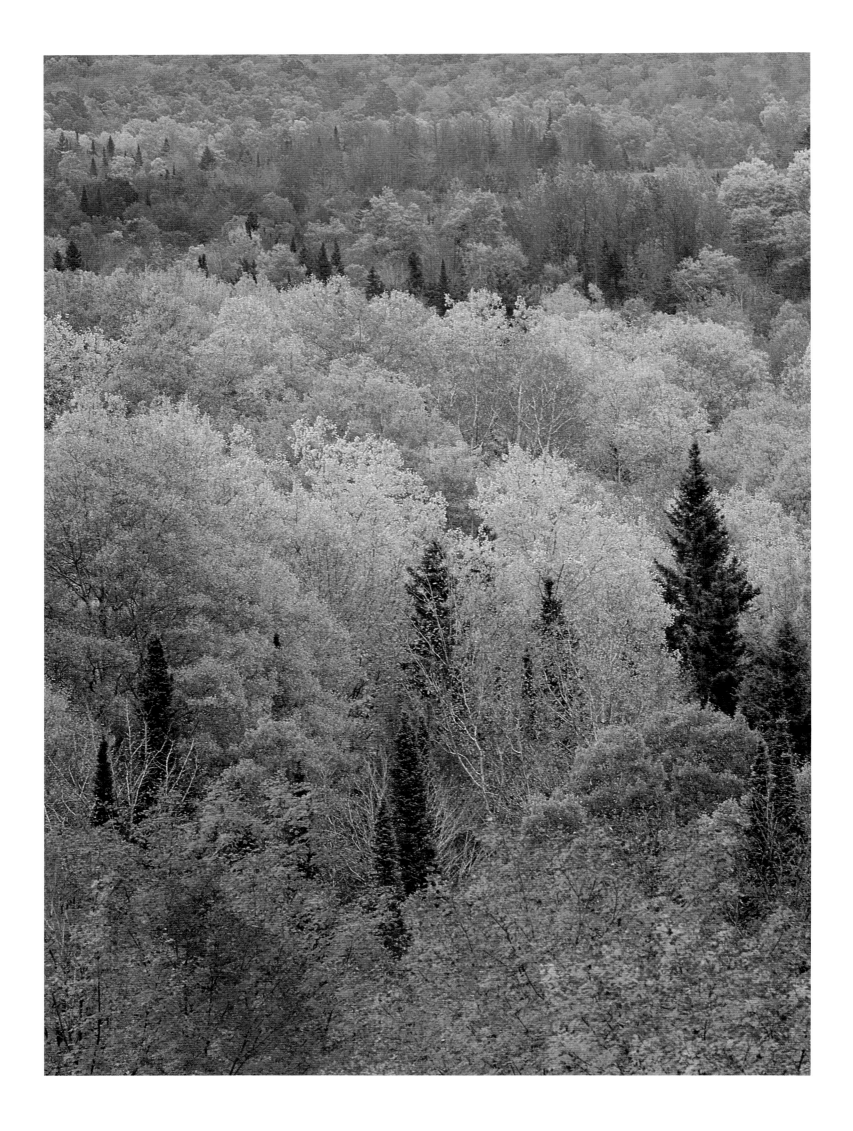

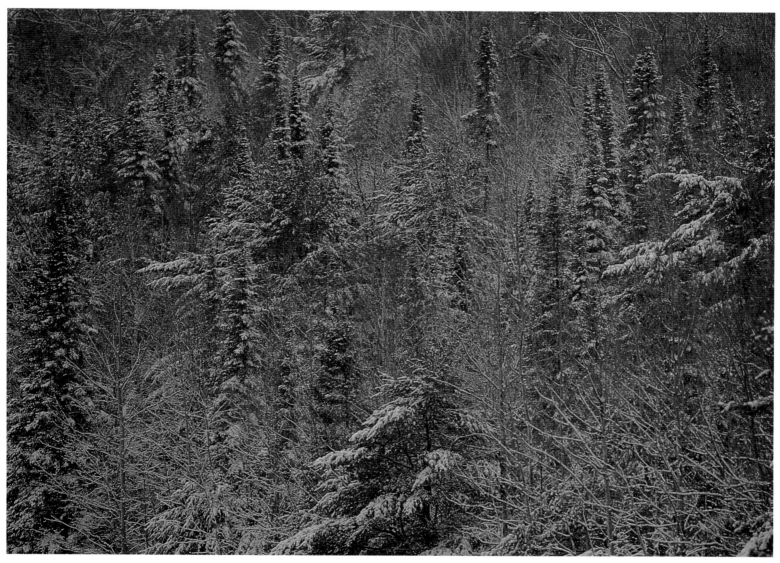

◄ The Penokee Hills are part of the Gogebic Iron Range, extending from Lake Superior's Michigan coast to Lake Namakagon. Relatively uninhabited until the discovery of iron ore deposits in the 1880s, the area soon boomed with more than fifty mines and "inexhaustible deposits." This unbridled prosperity survived less than a decade.
▲ Northeastern Wisconsin—the sparsely settled corner including Florence and Marinette counties—contains some of the wildest and grandest country in the state, including granite cliffs, iron ore hills, and immense forests where black bear and deer roam at will.

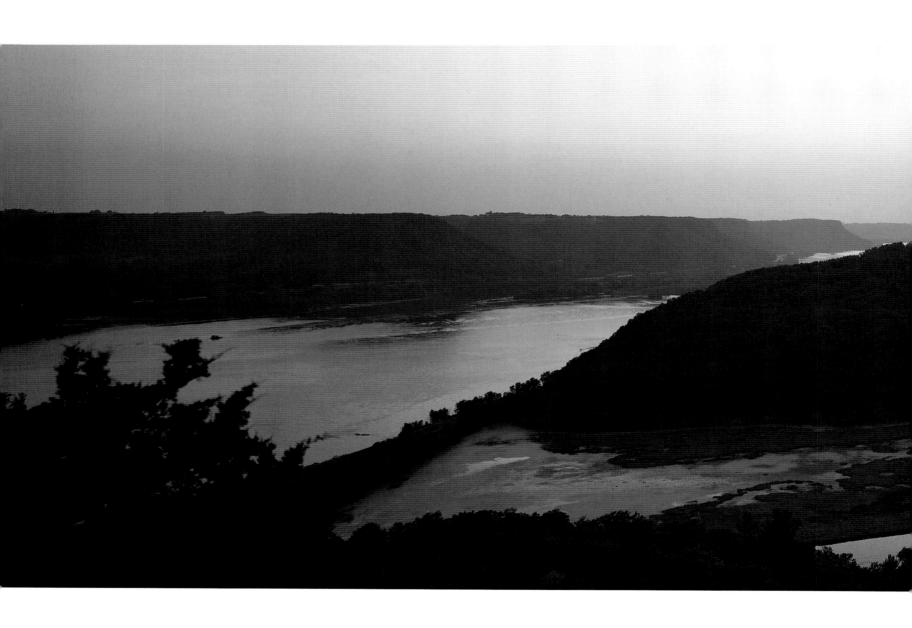

The Mississippi River is a river of history, of stories, and we are carried forward on its currents.

ROBERT E. GARD

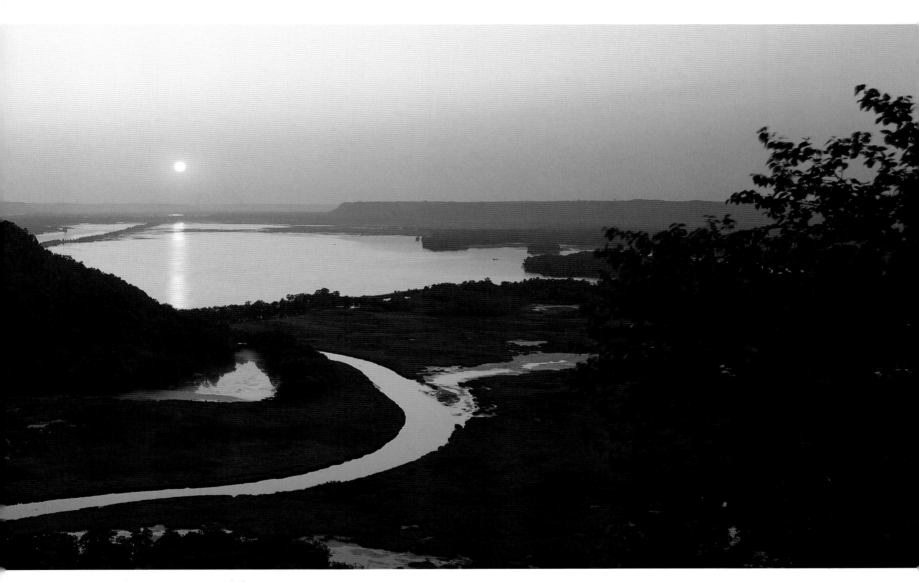

Trempealeau Mountain and the Mississippi River

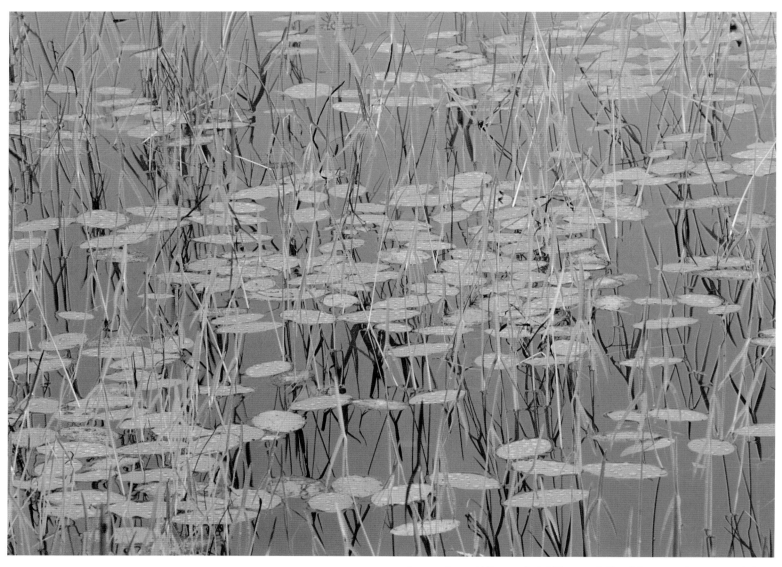

▲ In northern Wisconsin's Vilas and Oneida counties, more lakes, ponds, and bogs lie in close proximity than anywhere else in the world—all formed by the retreat of the last glacial ice mass.
► The Kickapoo River flows through several state wildlife areas that provide the wooded, swampy habitat preferred by the snowy egret. The Kickapoo is the longest river in the Driftless Area.
► ► One of the best prairie remnants in the Southeastern Moraine Natural Area, Young Prairie contains more than eighty species of native plants, including blazing star and three threatened species.

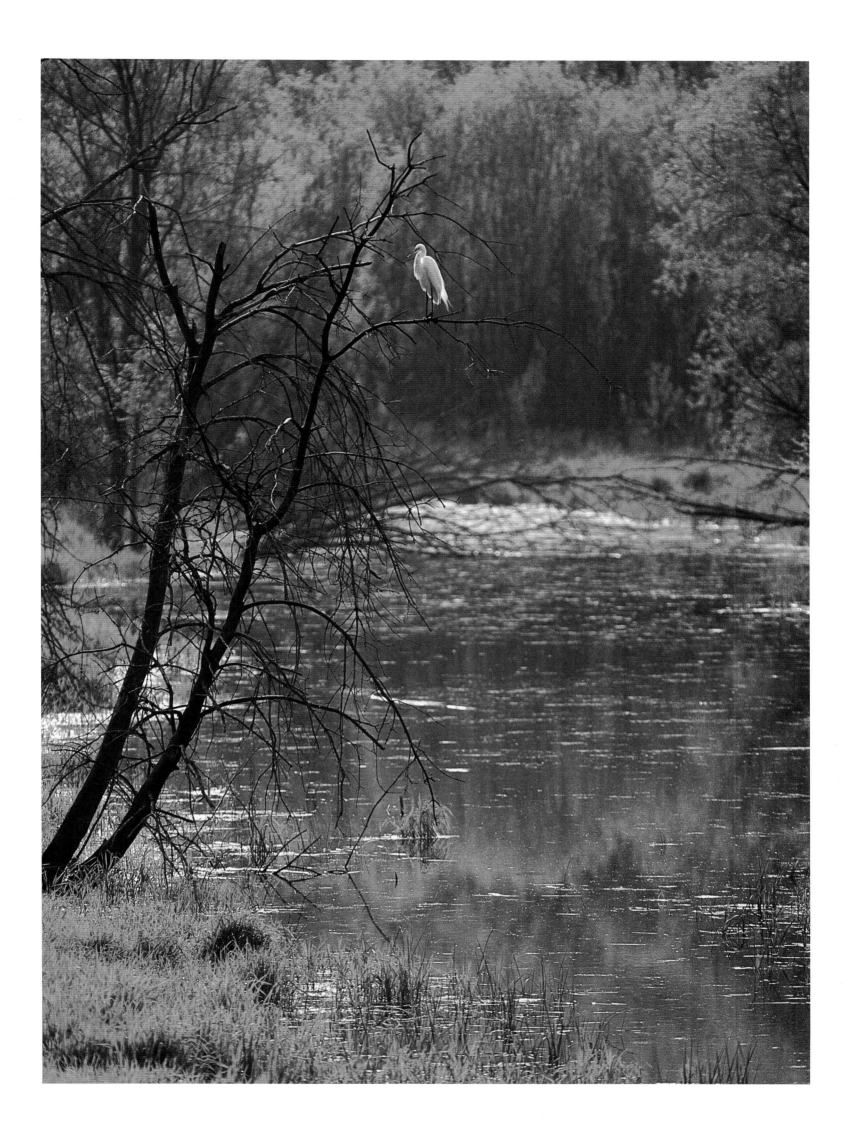

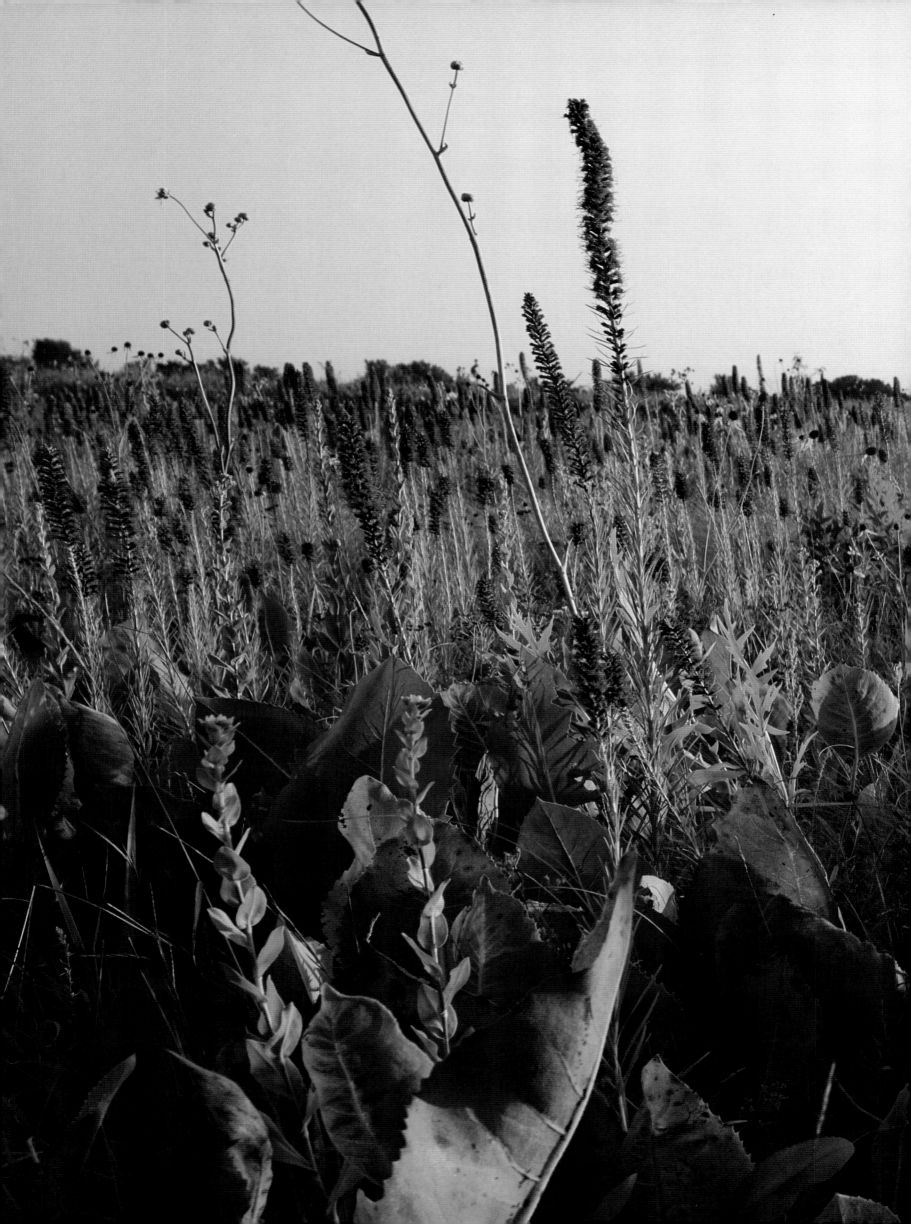

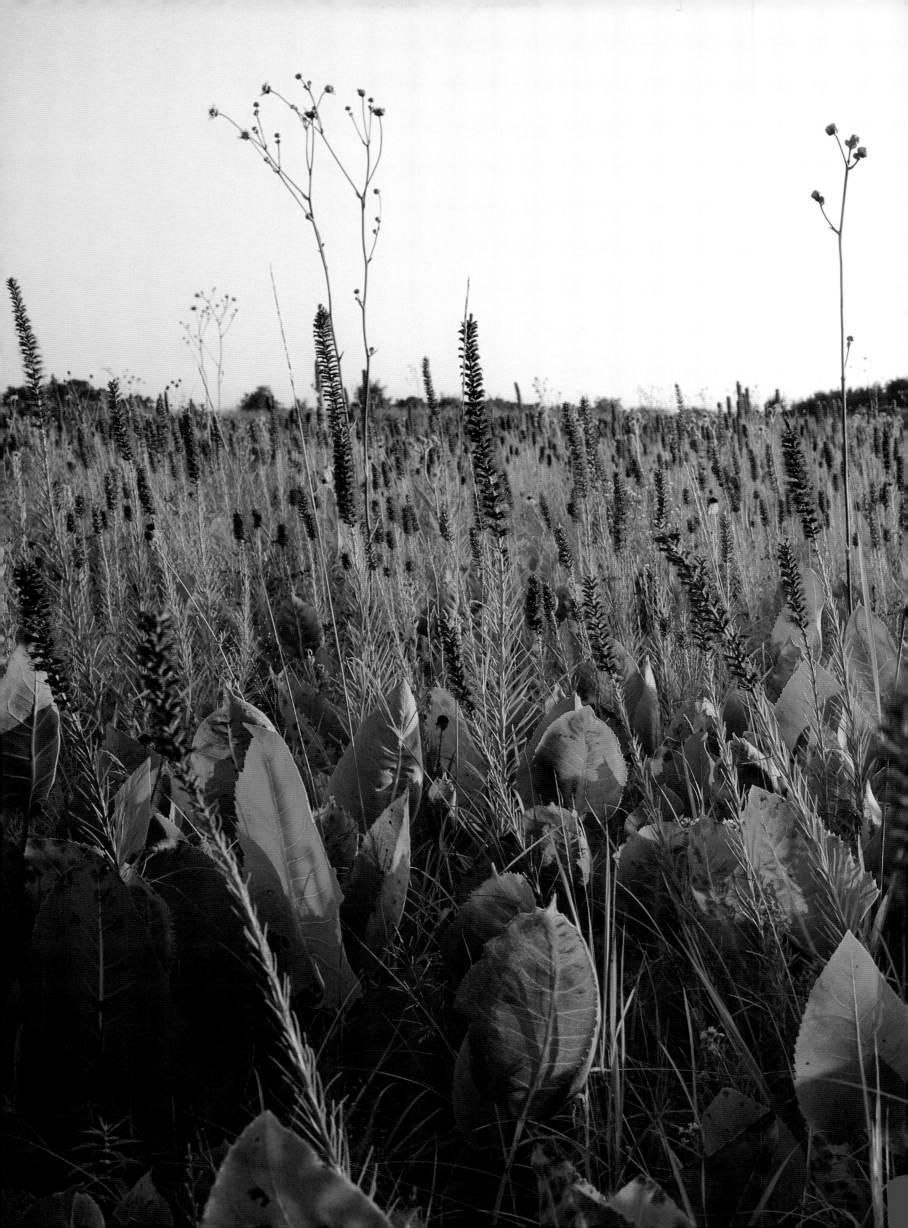

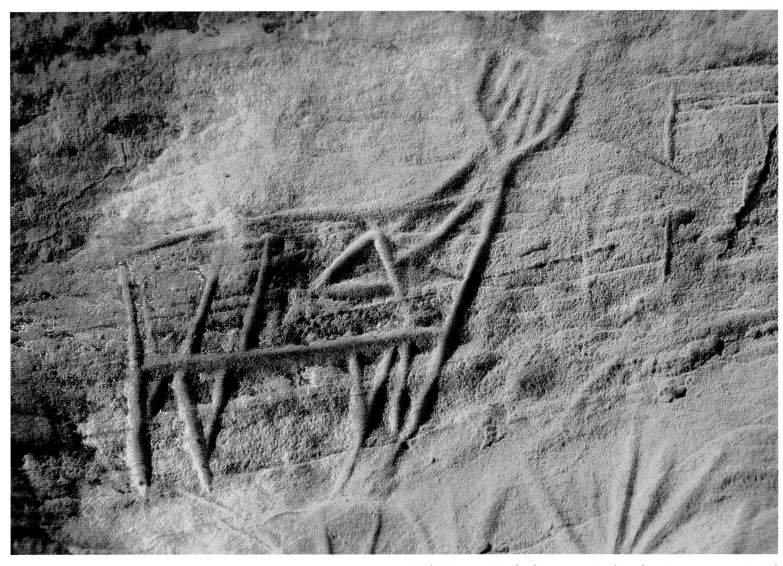

▲ Prehistoric petroglyphs, or excised rock art, are concentrated in the rugged Driftless Area of southwest Wisconsin, the only area of the state that was not leveled by glaciers during the Ice Age. ▶ Recently declared an endangered species, the eastern timber wolf numbers a mere twenty animals throughout the northern half of the state, all that remain from twenty thousand estimated to have lived statewide before settlement in the 1830s.

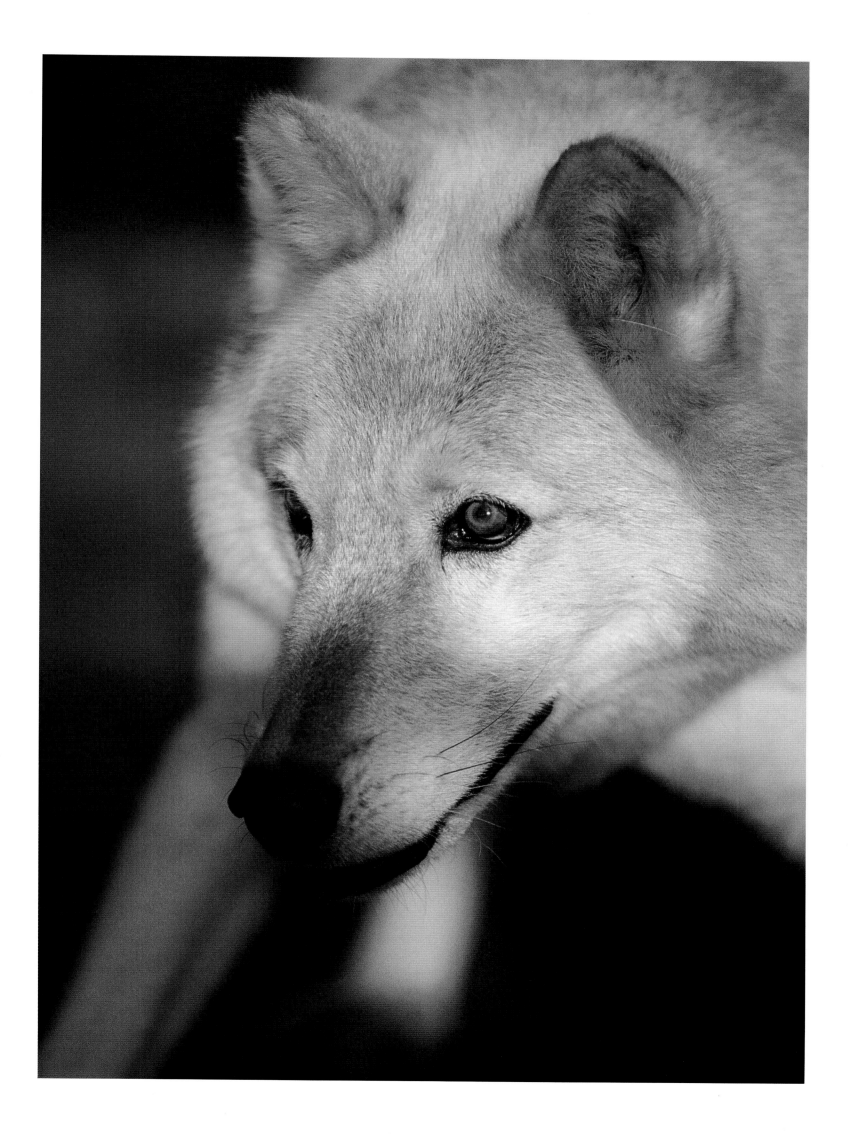

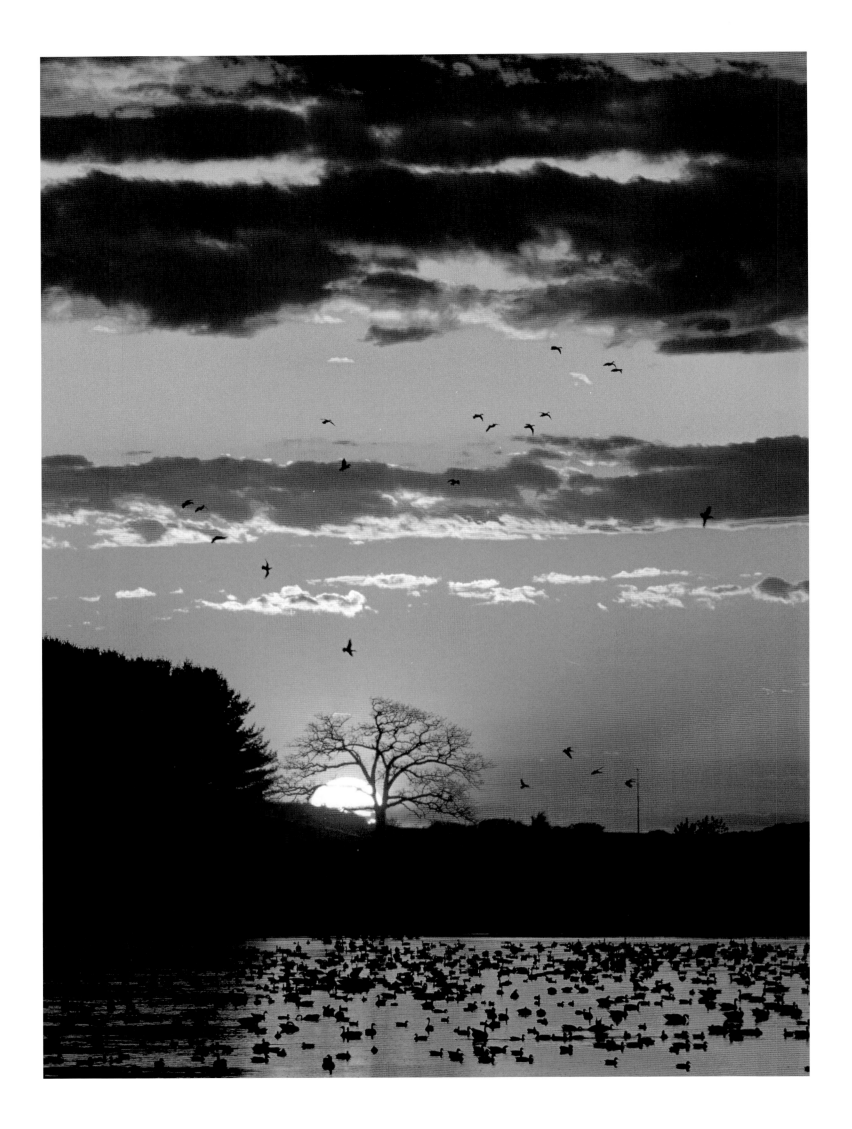

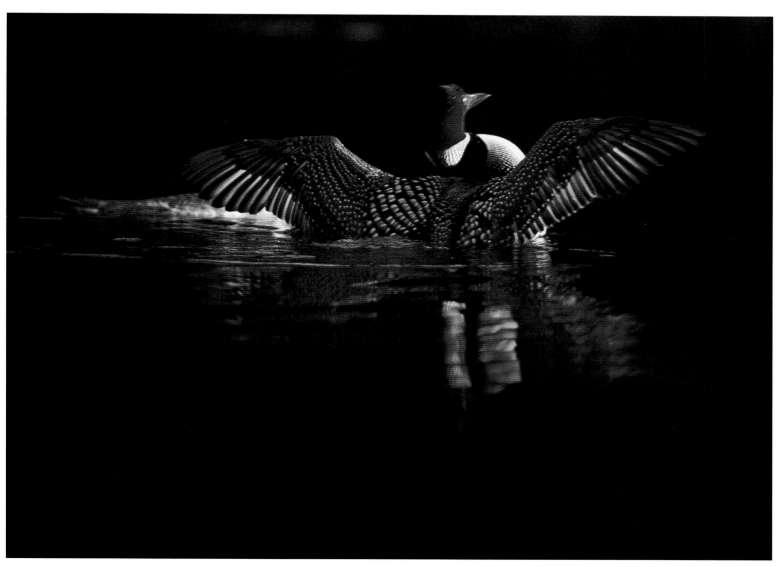

◄ Goose Pond in Columbia County is a small prairie pothole lake used by more than 240 bird species, primarily waterfowl and shorebirds—including tundra swans and eight species of ducks.
▲ For many people, witnessing the loon's stark beauty and unmistakable calls is part of Wisconsin's northwoods experience. Loons have been around for some twenty-five million years and are well adapted to their environment, yet less than three thousand make their summer home in Wisconsin today.

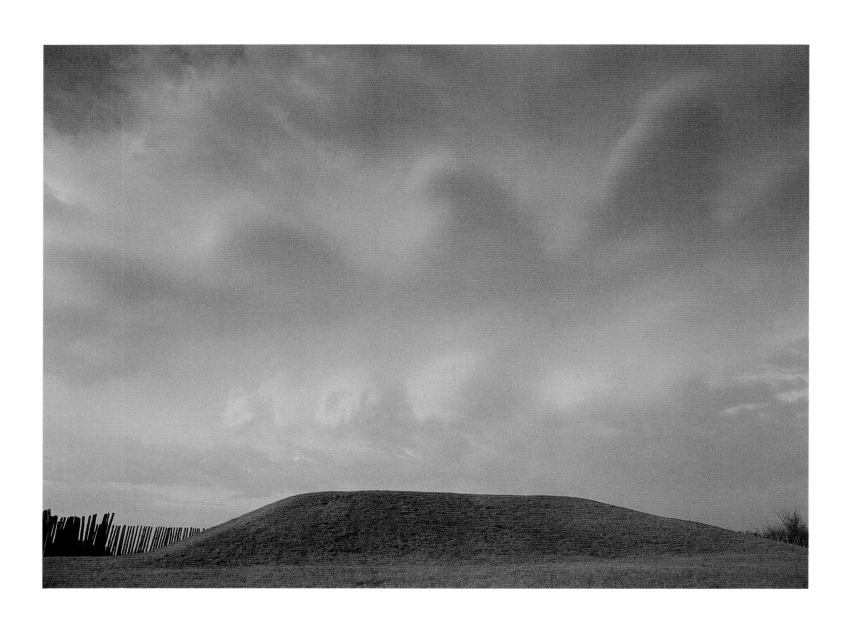

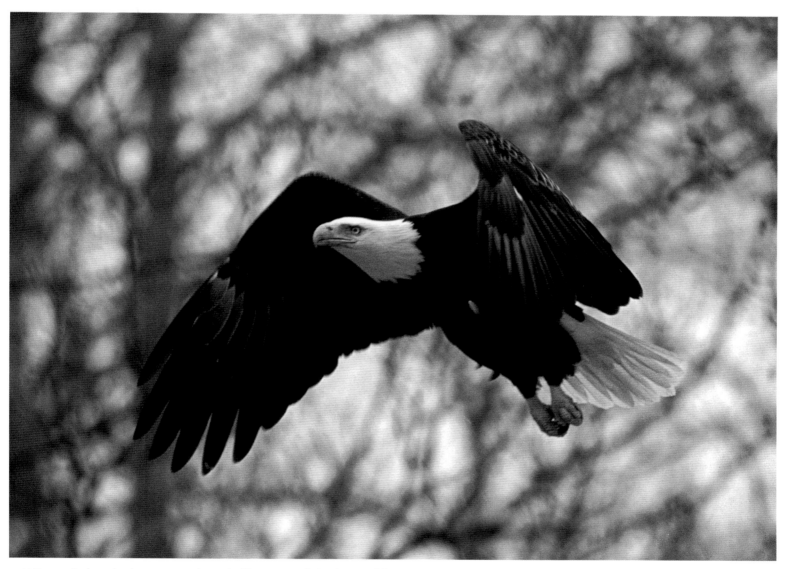

◄ Wisconsin has the largest number of effigy mounds in the world. Aztalan State Park housed a more advanced culture of approximately five hundred inhabitants around the year 1500. These mounds are thought to have served as a giant, precise calendar, as well as a site from which to observe the winter solstice sunrise.

▲ Though threatened, Wisconsin's bald eagle population continues to recover, with the number of breeding pairs increasing five-fold since 1970. The largest concentrations are in the northern third of the state, but most move south to open water along the Mississippi and Wisconsin rivers as the northern waters freeze.

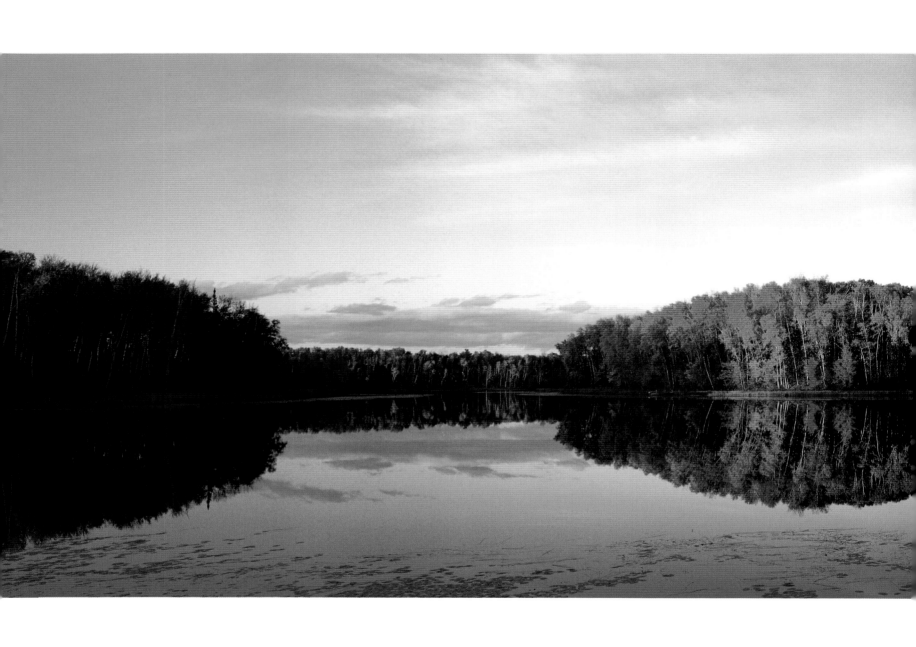

*Autumn is color, limitless color,
the very canvas of creation.*

OWEN J. GROMME

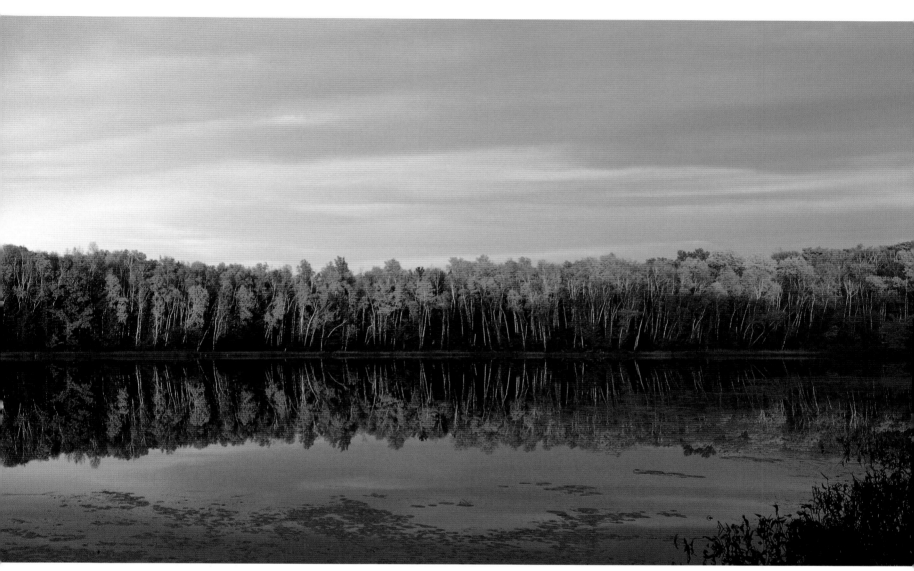

Twin Lakes, Bayfield County

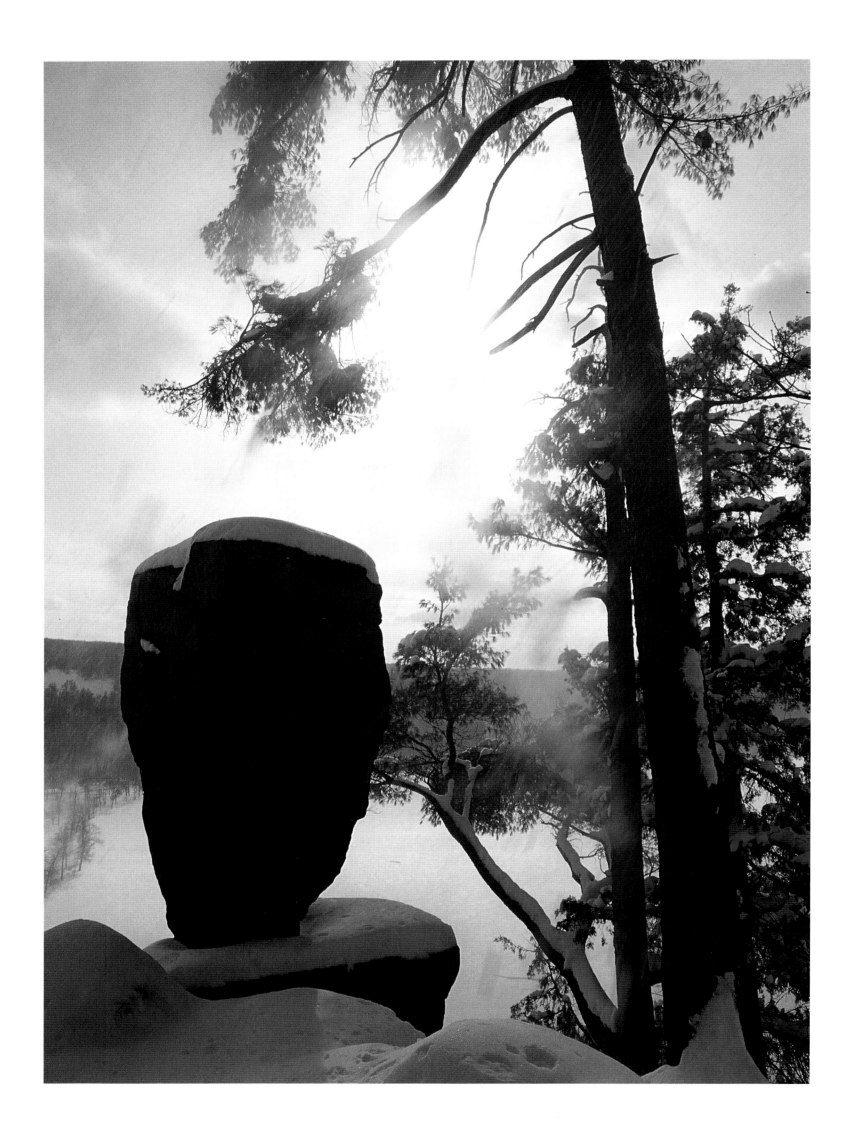

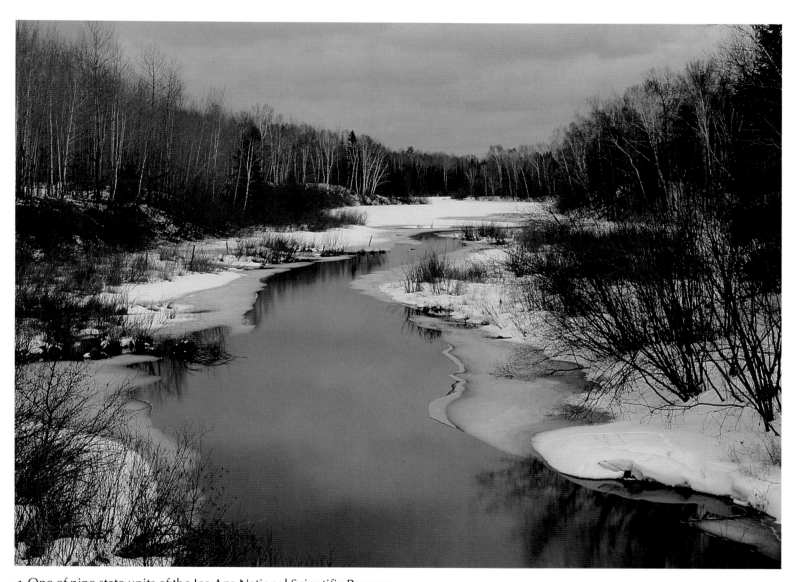

◄ One of nine state units of the Ice Age National Scientific Reserve, Devil's Lake was formed by glacial debris and meltwater. The Wisconsin River, cutting through the quartzite of the Baraboo Range, created the eight hundred-foot-deep gorge. Glacial action also whittled landmarks like Balance Rock from the rock ridge.
▲ The Chippewa River flows through the heart of the Chequamegon National Forest, a relatively old-growth mesic forest composed of cedar and hemlock, which covers more than 840,000 acres in northern Wisconsin. Segments of the North Country Trail and the Ice Age Trail pass through the Chequamegon.

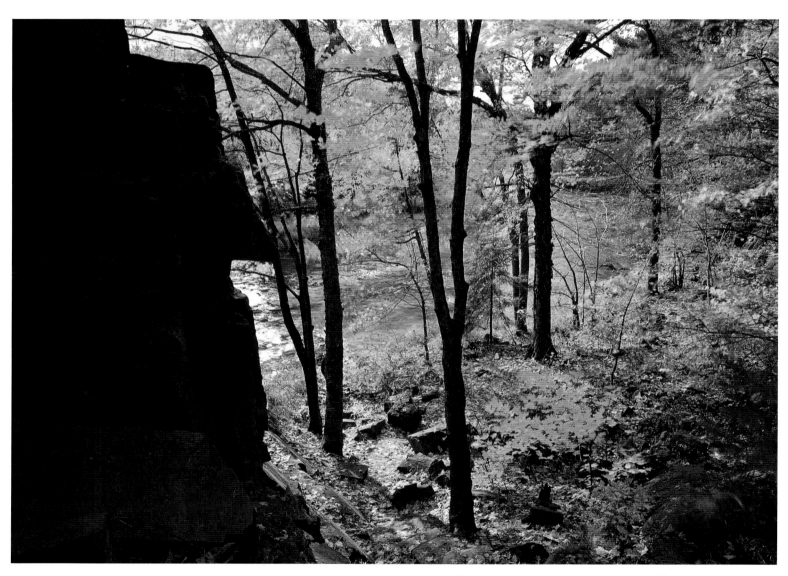

▲ In Marathon County near Wausau, the Dells of the Eau Claire River show a vertical bedrock tilt—caused by Precambrian geologic processes—along with cascades, stream terraces, and potholes.
▶ The white-tailed deer is Wisconsin's official wildlife animal and also its most abundant. Common throughout most areas of the state, its population has increased in the last decade to more than one million animals, due to loss of natural predators.

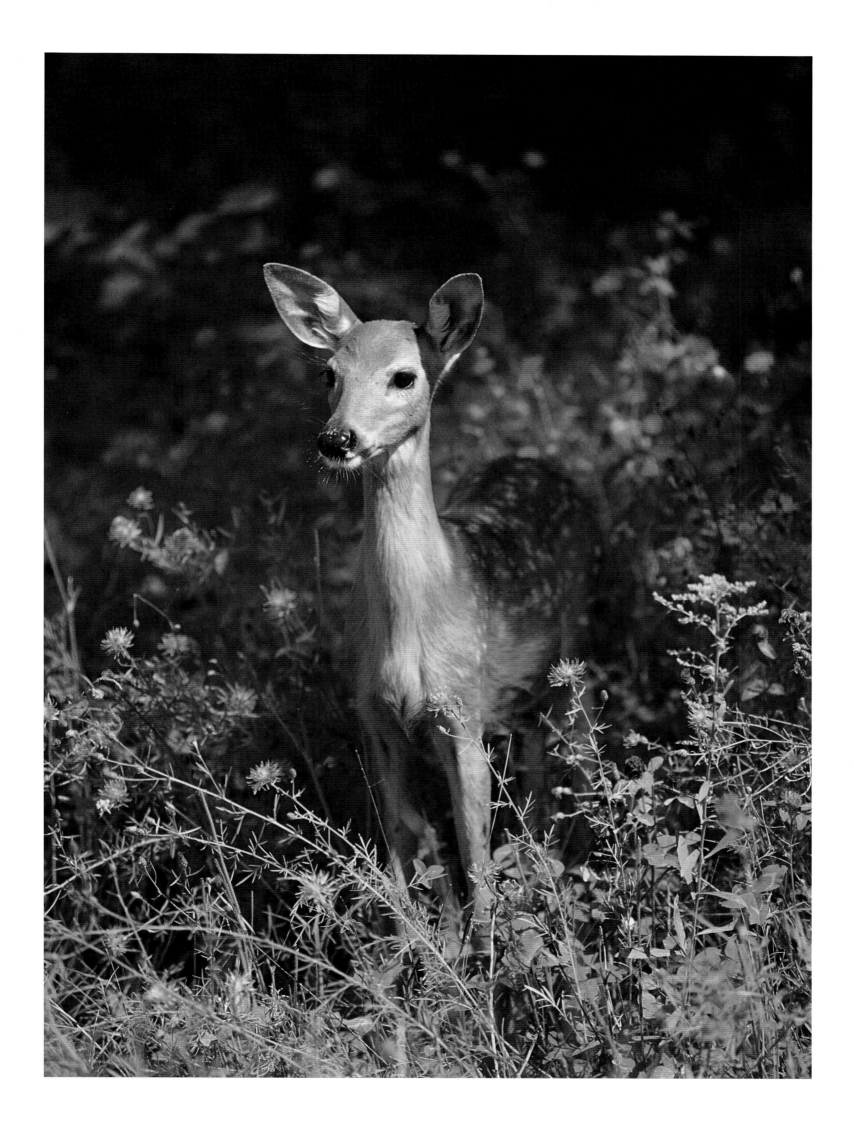

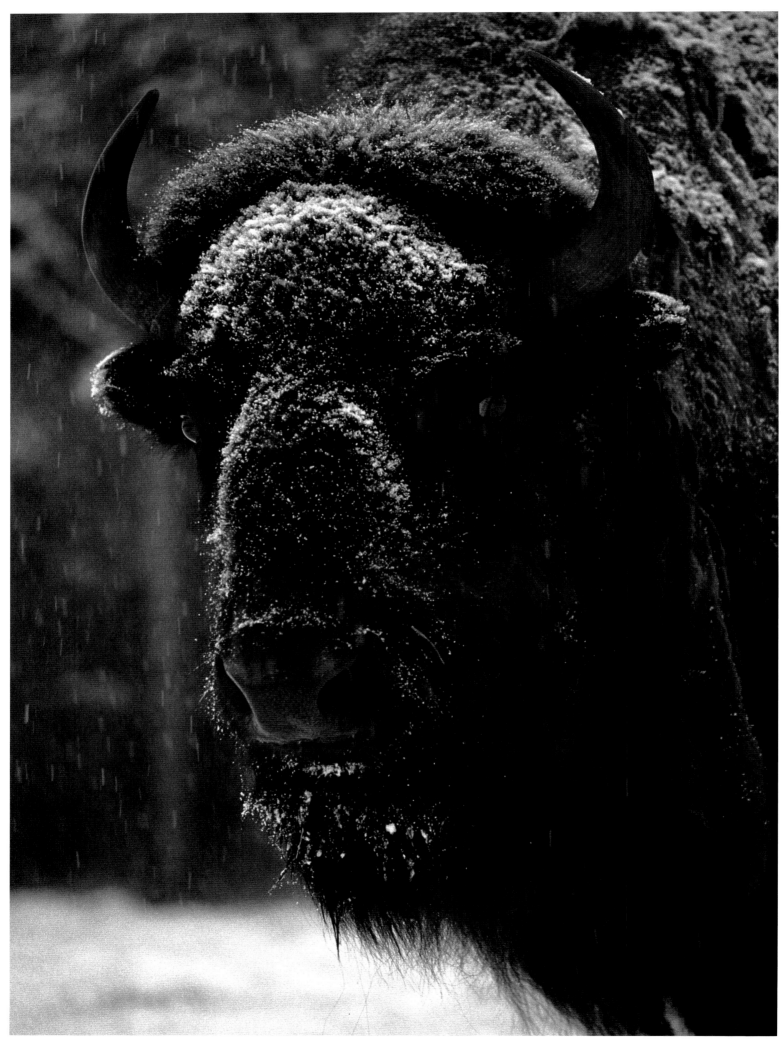

American bison, central Wisconsin

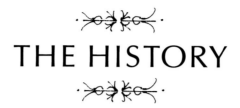

THE HISTORY

ORIGINAL INHABITANTS. The first people arrived in this land almost as soon as the last of the glaciers left, about eleven thousand years ago. Scientists speculate that the first inhabitants crossed into North America over the Bering Strait.

Anthropologists divide these first inhabitants into five major groups: the Old Copper Industry, the Woodland, the Hopewell, the Upper Mississippi, and the Middle Mississippi. Of these, the Woodland have left the most evidence of their way of life. Their descendants include the Menominee, Potawatomi, Chippewa, Fox, Sauk, Mascouten, and Kickapoo.

The Woodland Indians migrated to Wisconsin a thousand or more years ago, probably from the north. They made pottery (similar to pottery unearthed in Siberia), hunted game and fish, and gathered food in field and forest. Anthropologists believe they were the first to use the bow and arrow.

The richest cultural legacy left behind by the Woodland is their more than twelve thousand burial—or effigy—mounds, though not all are of Woodland origin. During the peak of the Woodland culture, burial mounds were constructed in the shapes of animals and birds, sometimes as humans, or simply as round or oblong shapes. They were seldom more than four feet high and were usually built on high ground near water. Concentrated in southern Wisconsin, more than two hundred are located in and around Madison alone.

During the Woodland period, several groups migrated into the state from the southeast. The Hopewellians brought stone knives and arrowheads, and polished stone and copper jewelry. Their relics suggest that they traveled widely and traded as far away as the Gulf of Mexico and into Mexico itself.

Today's Winnebagos are descendants of a later group, the Upper Mississippi people. They lived in permanent villages and carried on an advanced culture, much like the Hopewellians.

However, it was the Middle Mississippi people who were the most advanced group of immigrants. They were the builders of Aztalan, a large village of archaeological significance in southeastern Wisconsin (now a state park). The remains of this village show definite Mexican influence, leading to much speculation about Aztalan's history. Inside the village, which was enclosed with a high stockade fence, were three flat-topped pyramids, very similar to those found in ancient Mexico.

The invasion of the Europeans spelled the certain end of Native American dominance in Wisconsin. The Native Americans' last stand was with the Black Hawk war of 1832, certainly a shameful episode in American history. Black Hawk's little band of about a thousand Sauk and Fox, despite repeated attempts to surrender, was hunted down and massacred by American troops. After the brief war, only about 150 of Black Hawk's people remained.

EARLY EXPLORERS AND THE FUR TRADE. Historians say Jean Nicolet was the first white man to set foot in Wisconsin, crossing Lake Michigan and arriving on the east shore of Green Bay in 1634. Thinking he had arrived in China, he came wearing an ornate robe of China damask and carrying two guns, which he fired into the air upon landing. He must have made quite an impression on the Winnebagos who greeted him.

The explorers Groseilliers and Radisson made several forays into Wisconsin between 1656 and 1658. They were soon followed by the Jesuits, who hoped to convert many pagans to Christianity.

Rene Menard was the first priest to visit, followed by Claude Jean Allouez and then Father Jacques Marquette, who arrived in 1669. The Jesuits did not have great success in converting the Indians to Catholicism, but they did offer at least some protection to the Indians against the schemes of the fur traders and other European entrepreneurs.

When Nicolet landed at Green Bay, he was trying to find a western route to China, and was disappointed when he found the waters to be fresh and not salt. At the time, the Europeans thought of North America as little but a barrier to overcome on the way to the Orient. But Nicolet's visit had a far greater significance than he ever imagined. For the next two hundred years, fur—"soft gold"—was king in Upper Great Lakes.

European hat makers especially valued beaver hair, which made the very best felt. Since they had depleted the beaver population in Europe, pelts were scarce and prices high enough to attract a lively commerce in the New World. The French took the lead.

The tribes of the region profited greatly from the trade. As they said, "The beaver does everything well. It makes kettles, hatchets, knives, and bread. In short, it makes everything." They could trade beaver pelts not only for these items but also for fishing hooks, axes, traps, guns and gunpowder, cloth, ornamental jewelry, and other European goods to make their lives easier and better for attacking or defending themselves from their enemies.

The French controlled the fur trade until about 1763, when the British finally defeated them in Canada and took over all the French lands east of the Mississippi. After the British defeat in the War of 1812, the Americans seized control of the lucrative trade. After that, European styles changed and the demand for beaver pelts gradually diminished until about 1834, when the trade almost ended.

WESTWARD MOVEMENT. With the American victory in 1812, the Wisconsin territory began to attract permanent settlers. Miners settled around rich lead deposits in the southwest, near Mineral Point. Early farmers came to claim cheap or free land. Land speculators soon set up shop. Before long, lead mining took the place of fur trading as Wisconsin's primary industry.

Before this time, frontier Wisconsin was populated mostly by Native American tribes, fur traders, and soldiers. Lacking a local government, the territory was governed by the army, with major posts at Fort Howard at Green Bay, Fort Crawford at Prairie du Chien, and Fort Winnebago at Portage. The first hardy settlers lived near the forts for protection, but after Black Hawk's defeat in 1832, settlement accelerated greatly. Many new settlers came from New York and New England, spurred westward by intense competition for farmland in the East and facilitated by improved water and land routes. Government land offices opened in Green Bay, Mineral Point, and Milwaukee, selling good farmland for $1.25 an acre. In Europe, two male heirs might fight to the death over an acre of stony loam, but in America there seemed endless stretches of fertile black prairie, practically for the taking. Word spread quickly.

Wisconsin became a state in 1848, and the westward movement continued apace. Settlers arrived daily, by steamboat to the port of Milwaukee or to Prairie du Chien from the Mississippi River, and overland to every part of the state. Germans followed the Yankee settlers in waves, some seeking religious freedom; others, relief from military conscription and overpopulation. They brought with them highly developed skills in cabinet making, brewing, baking, and leather working. They brought superior German educational methods (the first American kindergarten was established in Wisconsin), and medical expertise. They also brought a work ethic that helped build prosperity.

With the Germans, or soon after, arrived the Norwegians, the Finns, Dutch, Irish, Welsh, Scotch, Jews from eastern Europe, Poles, Swiss, Danes, Belgians, and more. Between 1840 and 1890, most of the immigrants came from northern and western Europe. But starting in the 1880s, substantial numbers also arrived from southern and eastern Europe. By the beginning of the twentieth century the cultural composition of the state was fairly well set. Instead of a melting pot, which would homogenize all people, Wisconsin became a rich stew, each new group of immigrants adding to the texture and flavor.

AGRICULTURE. The original inhabitants of Wisconsin were not only expert hunters, trappers, and fishers, but they were also competent farmers. At the time of European contact, they were raising corn, beans, pumpkins, potatoes, squash, cucumbers, melons, and other crops to help see them through the winter. Although most writers described their agriculture as primitive, it was Native Americans who tended the land for centuries, and it was white settlers who migrated west because they had worn out their New England soils in only a few generations.

The Yankees or "Yorkers" from New York and New England were the first settlers to farm Wisconsin soils. Agriculture, established first to support the booming lead mining industry, took on an importance of its own after the lead boom died out before the Civil War. The Yankees grabbed all the prime prairie soils of the south, leaving poorer lands of the north to later immigrants. The northern timber lands were turned to agriculture only after loggers had made a thorough harvest. This "cutover country" was horribly difficult to clear, offering little more than a subsistence lifestyle for those who tried to claim it.

Dairy farming is the backbone of Wisconsin agriculture today, but for many years wheat was king. It began in the 1830s, and by the 1860s Wisconsin had risen to number two, behind Illinois, among the states in wheat production. Milwaukee and Chicago vied with each other for position as the world's number one wheat shipping port. King Wheat, however, was riding for a fall. In the late 1870s and early 1880s, plant diseases and exhausted soil resulted in several bad growing seasons. Finally, the arrival of the dread chinch bug, which had a voracious appetite for wheat, spelled the death of the king.

Under the urging of the state agricultural college, Wisconsin farmers traded in the plow for the cow. Dairy farming had been increasing for some time in the state, partly because of the expertise of the Swiss immigrants around New Glarus, and the state university took the lead in improving the techniques of cheese and butter production. Wisconsin soon became preeminent in dairy production, a position it continues to hold today. Although

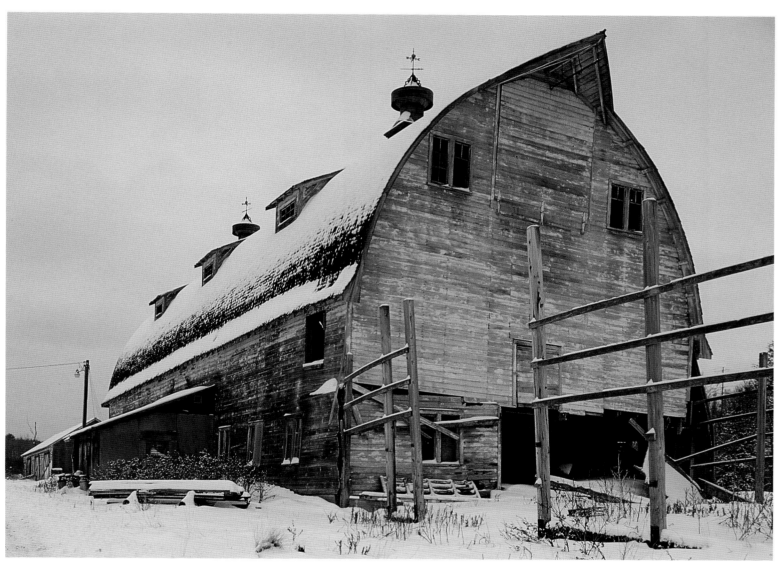

Because of its varied and bountiful background of ethnic and national origins, Wisconsin possesses an architectural heritage of exceptional historic significance. Appropriate materials, solid fundamental design, and quality workmanship were characteristic of the great majority of old Wisconsin buildings.

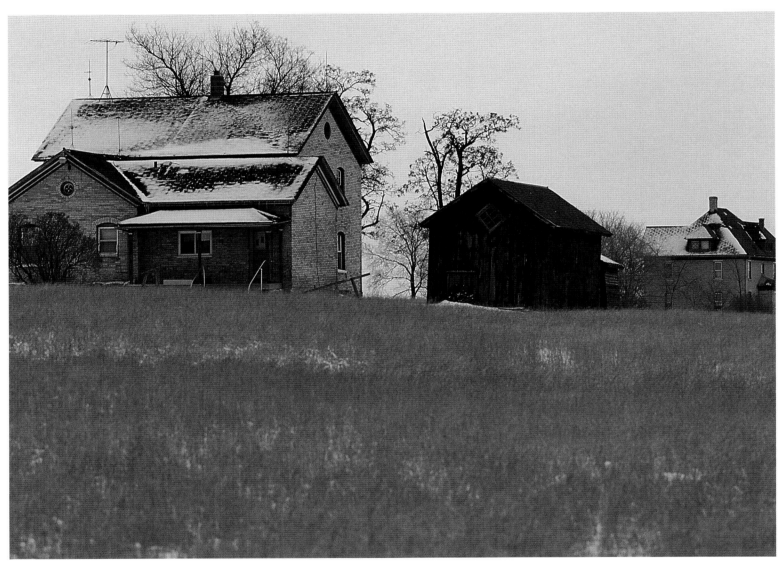

While much of the commonplace dominated both the rural and urban setting, the early architecture of Wisconsin had a character that reflected the forces at work in pioneer lives—tradition, invention, utility, adaptation, and fashion.

California has challenged Wisconsin in total dairy production, all car license plates in Wisconsin still proudly proclaim it as "The Dairy State."

Besides its role in dairy production, Wisconsin today ranks number one among states in the production of sweet corn, green peas, and snap beans for processing; corn for silage; and mink pelts. It also ranks number two in oat and cranberry production, and number three in hay and potato production. Wisconsin's strong agriculture, along with its industrial base and tourism industry, provides a balanced economy for dependable growth.

LOGGING. At the time of European contact, Wisconsin had the largest concentration of pine forest in the nation. Magnificent white pines, in addition to cedar, spruce, hemlock, and hardwood trees, virtually carpeted the northern two-thirds of the state. The experts believe the Chippewa River Valley alone once had one-sixth of the nation's white pine. In all, Wisconsin had an estimated 130 billion board feet of white pine.

In a single century, all this was destroyed, the result of the voracious appetite for lumber created by westward expansion—and a greed seldom equaled in human history.

Commercial lumbering had been going on in Wisconsin since the early part of the nineteenth century. The supply of pine was seemingly without limit, and the vast network of rivers provided ideal routes for moving the logs to market. The Wisconsin, Black, Wolf, Chippewa, and St. Croix rivers were the most active in carrying logs. Later in the century, when the westward migration increased the need for lumber, and when railroads provided a transportation alternative to water, lumbering became more profitable than ever. The railroads themselves used prodigious amounts of lumber for ties, fuel, and building bridges and boxcars.

In the first two-thirds of the century, lumbering flourished on a relatively small scale. But railroad expansion allowed easy access to deeper forests and the marketing of Wisconsin pine to all parts of the nation. The lumber boom was on, an "Empire in Pine" seized by lumber barons and giant corporations, who wielded considerable economic and political power.

The number of trees removed from the forests of Wisconsin increased annually until the peak year of 1892, when an estimated four billion board feet were sold. So careless was the harvest that an estimated 40 percent of usable lumber was left behind to rot or burn. Wisconsin continued to lead the nation in the production of white pine lumber until the end of the century. Then, the supply at last diminished and the forests cut over and abandoned, the lumber barons moved on to new forests in the South and Pacific Northwest.

Travelers today can get the flavor of the old logging camps by visiting one of Wisconsin's many logging museums, scattered throughout the former pine forests. Some of the best are the Camp Five Logging Museum in Laona, Empire in Pine Museum in Downsville, the Logging Museum on Stephenson Island, and the Rhinelander Logging Museum.

COMMERCIAL FISHING. Wisconsin's water resources have long provided fish for its human inhabitants. The seventeenth-century Jesuit priests write glowingly of piscatory abundance, describing unbelievably large specimens of sturgeon, trout, and whitefish in Lake Michigan. Clear-running streams provided a wealth of trout, while small lakes yielded bass, sturgeon, pike, muskellunge, and panfish. Fish provided a major part of the diet of the Indian peoples for centuries. The voyageurs depended greatly on fish for daily sustenance, as did early settlers throughout the state.

While some entrepreneurs looked to the pine forests as potential sources of wealth, others looked to Lake Michigan. As early as 1836, a commercial fishery was established at Two Rivers. Detroit was a major purchaser of Lake Michigan fish, using two thousand barrels annually. Chicago and Milwaukee experienced solid population growth in the 1860s and 1870s, creating greater markets for the abundant whitefish. In 1872, more than 3,750 tons of Lake Michigan fish moved through the Chicago markets. Within three years, the total had grown to six thousand tons. Still the demand grew unabated, until in 1880 more than eleven thousand tons of fish were harvested and routed through Chicago to the entire Midwest.

Green Bay was the center of commercial fishing in Wisconsin. In winter, with the waters of Green Bay frozen over, fishermen erected hundreds of ice shanties, so they could catch and ship fresh fish to market year-round.

By 1885, the whitefish population had dropped drastically and showed no signs of reviving. Again, human greed and the failure to protect the resource spelled the end of prosperity. As the whitefish declined further, fishing became more intensive. Only 3,250 tons were caught in 1885, and by 1940 the total had dropped to 375 tons.

With the decline of the whitefish, fishermen began to concentrate their efforts on trout and herring. Sturgeon, once considered a trash fish, became popular for its yield of caviar—so popular, in fact, that it was nearly extinct by the 1930s.

Lake Michigan continued to yield impressive tonnages of fish, but these were largely alewives, used for pet food, and chubs instead of the preferred whitefish and trout. Further devastation came with the introduction of the sea lamprey in 1934. This eel-like fish attaches its mouth to larger fish and sucks its blood until it kills the host. The lamprey decimated populations of both whitefish and trout, and decimated the Lake Michigan fishing industry in the process.

For most of the twentieth century, the Wisconsin state government, along with the governments of surrounding states, has tried through careful regulation, stocking, and fish management programs to preserve the fisheries resources of the Great Lakes. Today, commercial and sport anglers share the resource of the Great Lakes, while sportsmen count Wisconsin's inland lakes, rivers, and streams as among the nation's finest fishing spots.

INDUSTRY AND MANUFACTURING. Oscar Mayer hot dogs. Parker pens. Weyerhaeuser paper. Kleenex. Schlitz, Miller, and Pabst Blue Ribbon beer. Little Golden Books. Hamilton Beach kitchen appliances. Johnson Wax. Hotpoint dishwashers. Harley-Davidson motorcycles. Duncan Yo-Yos. Ray-O-Vac batteries. A-C spark plugs. John Deere tractors. West Bend cooking pots. Briggs & Stratton engines. Kohler bathroom fixtures. The beloved Nash

Rambler. Many Wisconsin products are known throughout the nation and the world, though their users might not connect them with Wisconsin.

Wisconsinites have always been an inventive people, too. The outboard engine was invented here. And the typewriter. And the snowmobile, the automobile speedometer, and the threshing machine. Resulting from the hospitable land and ample water resources, combined with the industrious nature of the European immigrants, industry and manufacturing have always been an important part of the Wisconsin occupational mix.

Even in pre-statehood days when there were no cities, industry took root. Not surprisingly, sawmills were among the first enterprises to spring up, but an 1840 census also shows commercial manufacture, though slight, of candles, soap, beer, wax, and hats. Gristmills soon sprang up for the milling of wheat, mushrooming in the mid-eighteenth century as wheat became the state's major product, second only to lumber in total production value.

Papermaking developed mainly in the Fox River Valley, and by 1960 had grown to be the state's fourth-largest industry. As a natural consequence, with a nearby supply of paper, printing also became a major industry. Plywood and other wood products also play an important role, owing much to the United States Forest Products Laboratory, a research institution located in Madison.

Wisconsin produced many supplies—tanks, trucks, motorcycles, landing craft, ships, submarines, bulldozers, shell casings, and cannons—for World War I and World War II efforts.

Today, Wisconsin continues its strong industrial tradition as it seeks a new place in the post-industrial economy. Education will play a great part in this effort, and Wisconsin is fortunate to have an excellent public school system and one of the nation's foremost university systems.

RAILROADS. Wisconsinites have had a love-hate relationship with railroads since the beginning. In the last century, when the promised railroads offered easy transportation of crops and great profits, Wisconsin farmers eagerly mortgaged their farms for a bit of railroad stock and a bagful of promises. Often, the promised tracks never materialized, stock issues were fraudulent, railroad barons set rates so high farmers could not use them to send crops to market, and the crooked politicians were securely in the barons' pockets. All this hanky-panky led to the Granger Laws, which were early attempts to regulate railroad rates, and eventually to true government regulation that has continued until this day.

The first rail line in the state, opened in 1851, ran between Milwaukee and Waukesha. The Milwaukee & Mississippi line continued to build westward, reaching Madison in 1854, and Prairie du Chien on the Mississippi River in 1857. Another line, between Milwaukee and La Crosse, was completed the following year. Before long, north-south routes also became realities. But many citizens resented the railroad promoters' slick and often dishonest means of financing construction. Between 1850 and 1857, six thousand Wisconsin farmers mortgaged their farms to the tune of nearly five million dollars, all to buy railroad stock. That stock became worthless during the panic of 1857, in which every railroad in Wisconsin went bankrupt, but eastern bankers still demanded payment on the mortgages. A great hue and cry went up across Wisconsin. The legislature passed fourteen laws to release farmers from their debt obligations, but the state Supreme Court held them all to be unconstitutional. Farmers across the state organized into clubs to fight the railroads and the eastern bankers, vowing never to give up their homes without a bloody fight. German farmers in Ozaukee and Washington counties destroyed several railroad bridges, a depot, and some track. Eventually, the bankers canceled most of the mortgages, but relations between the railroads and the ordinary people of Wisconsin were never the same again.

By the time of the Civil War, Wisconsin's rail lines totaled 891 miles. After the war, rails were laid at a quicker pace than ever, until by 1890 the total was 5,583 miles, and by the outbreak of World War I Wisconsin's rail lines totaled 7,963 miles.

But that was to be the peak of railroad building in Wisconsin. Increasingly strict government regulation and, especially after World War II, stronger labor unions and competition from motor vehicles led to the railroads' decline. By 1989, only 4,420 miles of track remained, and more lines are being abandoned every year, some made into recreational trails for bicycles and snowmobiles.

WISCONSIN AND THE CIVIL WAR. When the first shots were fired on Fort Sumter, in 1861, Wisconsin had been a state for only thirteen years. The people were eager to prove themselves loyal members of the Union, and they quickly rallied to support the Union cause. Governor Alexander Randall pledged the state's entire resources to the war effort.

More than ninety-one thousand Wisconsin men responded to the call; nearly twelve thousand paid with their lives. The state sent fifty-six regiments to the cause, training recruits at Fond du Lac, Milwaukee, and Racine, but mainly at Madison, where the State Fair Grounds became a training camp.

Wisconsin troops fought in every major battle, distinguishing themselves many times over. The most famous Wisconsin unit was the Iron Brigade, which was made up of the Second, Sixth, and Seventh Wisconsin Volunteers, plus the Nineteenth Indiana and the Twenty-fourth Michigan. The Iron Brigade fought in the Army of the Potomac and suffered heavy losses at Gettysburg. The Wisconsin Fifteenth Infantry, from a Norwegian-American area, had 899 men, 115 of whom carried the name Ole. The Eighth Wisconsin, known as the Eagle Regiment, went into battle with a live bald eagle, "Old Abe," standing proudly (it is said) on a perch displaying the American flag.

Although most Wisconsin people supported the war, there were also many dissenters, including German intellectuals in the Milwaukee area. Draft resistance was high in the German areas, which is not surprising since many Germans immigrated to America to escape compulsory military service.

The war, while taking away many young Wisconsin men, also brought a certain measure of prosperity to the state. Great Lakes shipping was revived, and Milwaukee became the primary wheat shipping port in the nation. Factories turned out an endless stream of war materials. Wheat farming and lumbering flourished, and industry reached for new growth. Despite its heavy and tragic losses, Wisconsin emerged as a proud and energized new state, ready to take its place in the industrial age.

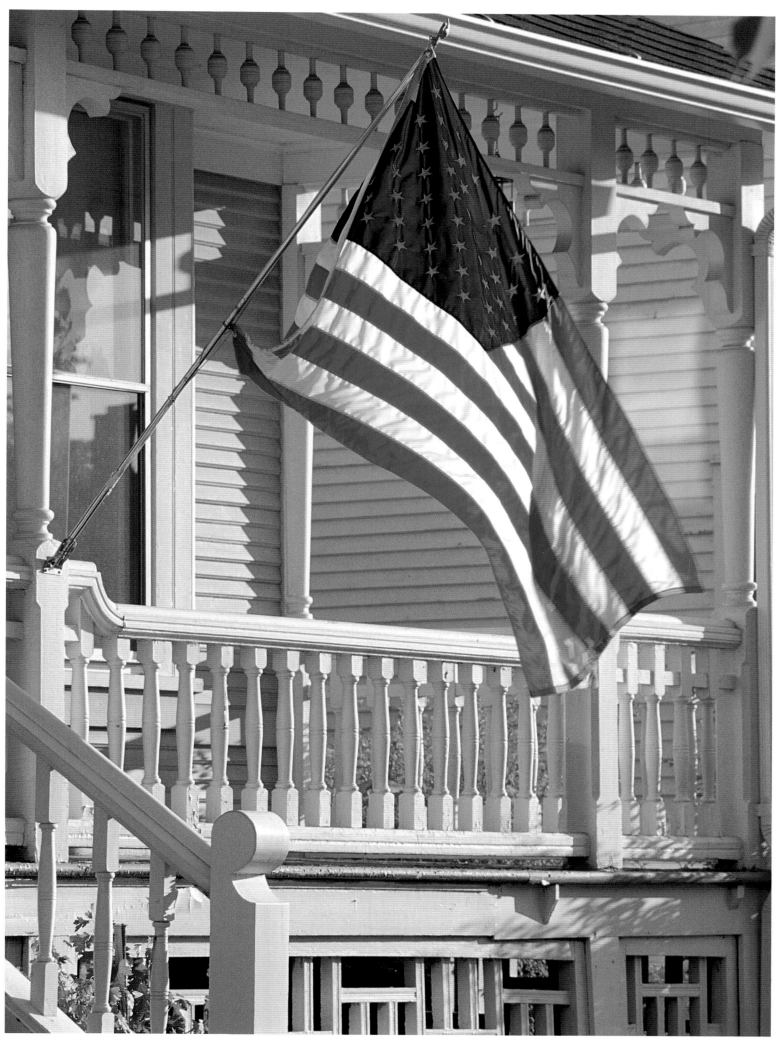

Fourth of July, Fond du Lac

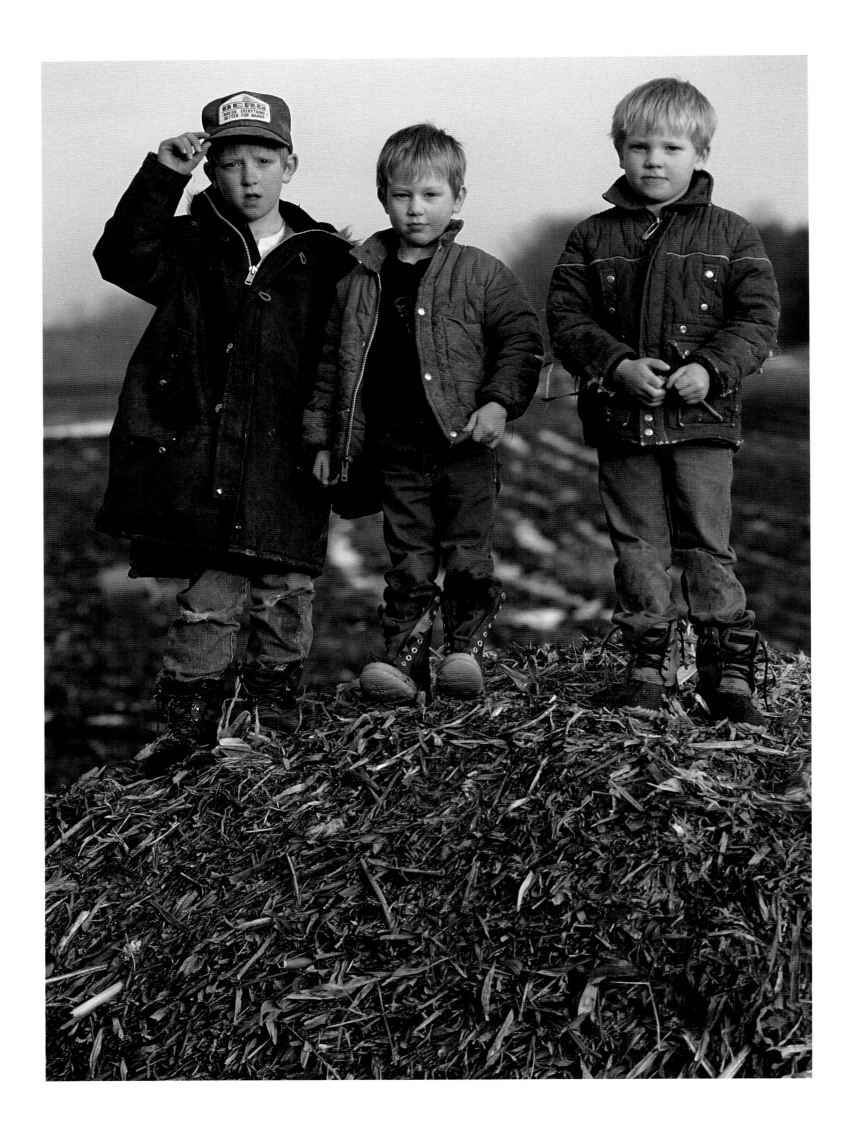

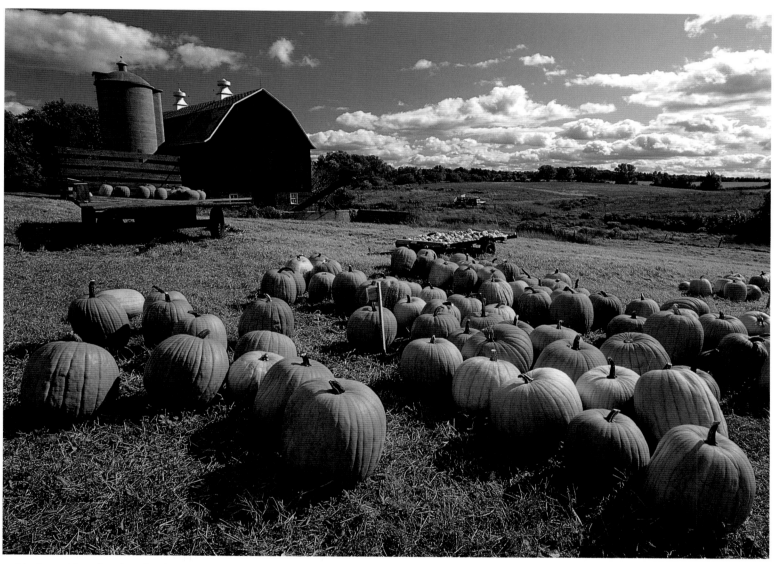

◄ Nationwide, the family farm has struggled against economic difficulty. While Wisconsin is no exception, the family farm realizes a degree of insulation from this decline by virtue of the dairy cow and the great variety of by-products from the milk industry.
▲ Autumn brings an abundance to Wisconsin's roadside stands and farmers markets, with a diverse harvest that ranges from potatoes to apples, pumpkins to cranberries, and ginseng to hickory nuts.

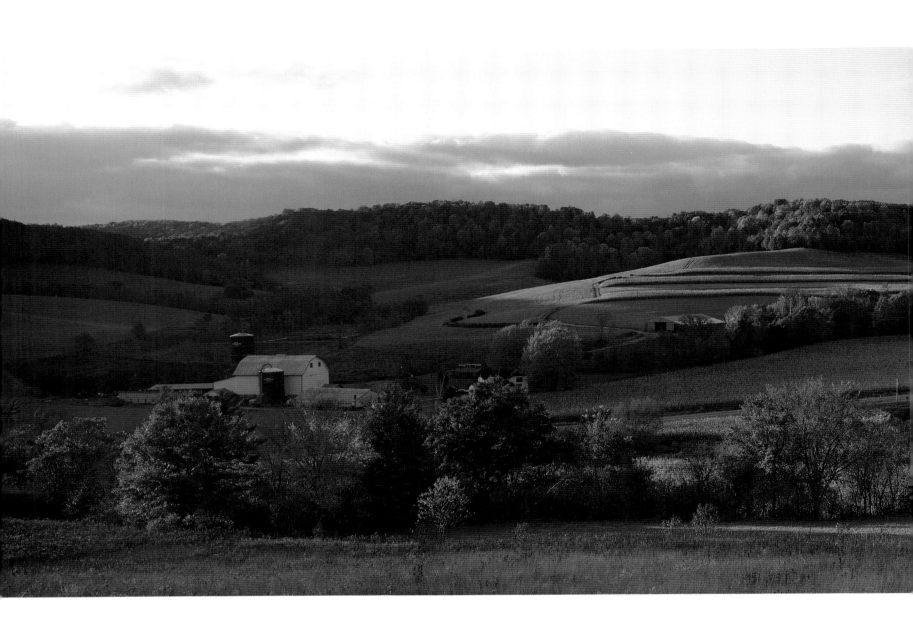

A valley farm, in the heart of the Driftless Region, where my heart can drift, down roads, past barns, into my childhood.

ROBERT E. GARD

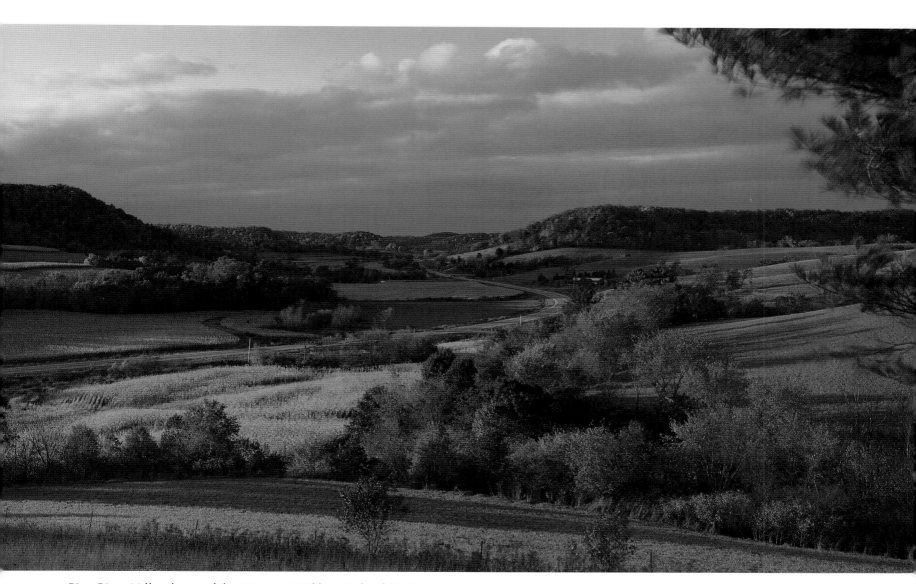

Pine River Valley, heart of the Western Driftless Upland Region

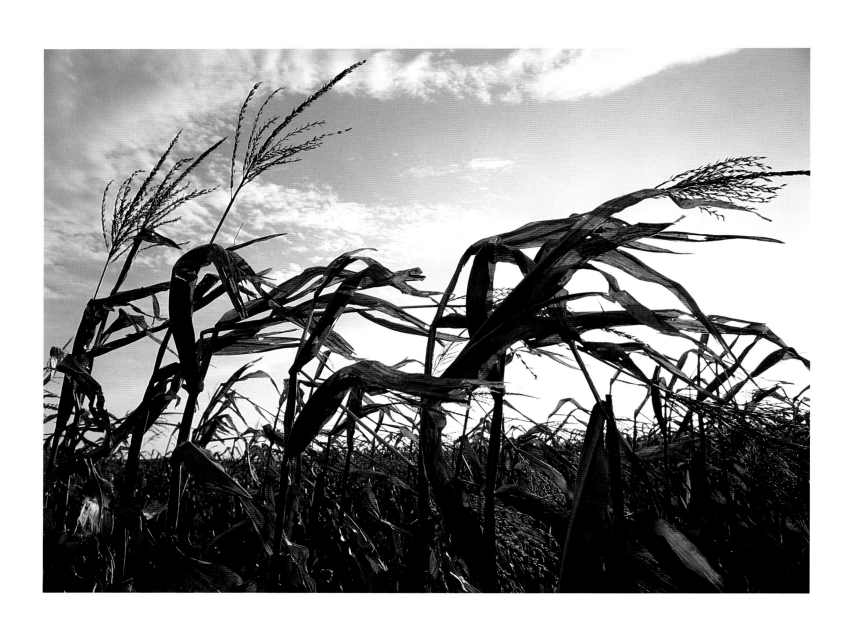

◄ With the southeastern corner of the state falling within the corn belt, Wisconsin ranks first in the nation in the production of corn for grain and silage, and in canned production for export.
▲ If the essence of a state is found in the beauty of its landscape, Wisconsin must be one of the most lovely. Whether natural or cultivated, beauty abounds in Wisconsin, and variety is its hallmark.

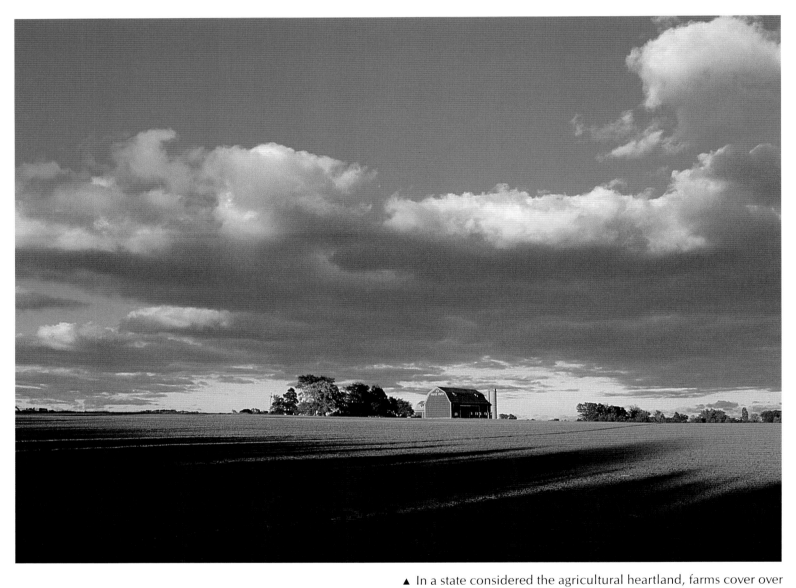

▲ In a state considered the agricultural heartland, farms cover over half of Wisconsin's total land area. Farms in the Lake Michigan Lowlands are known for their rich soil and longer growing season.
▶ At first thought of as the "general purpose cow" to provide milk, meat, and labor, the Holstein has become the symbol of Wisconsin's dairy industry. With more than one and one-half million dairy cows, Wisconsin, the nation's thirteenth-largest state, ranks first in milk, butter, and total cheese production.

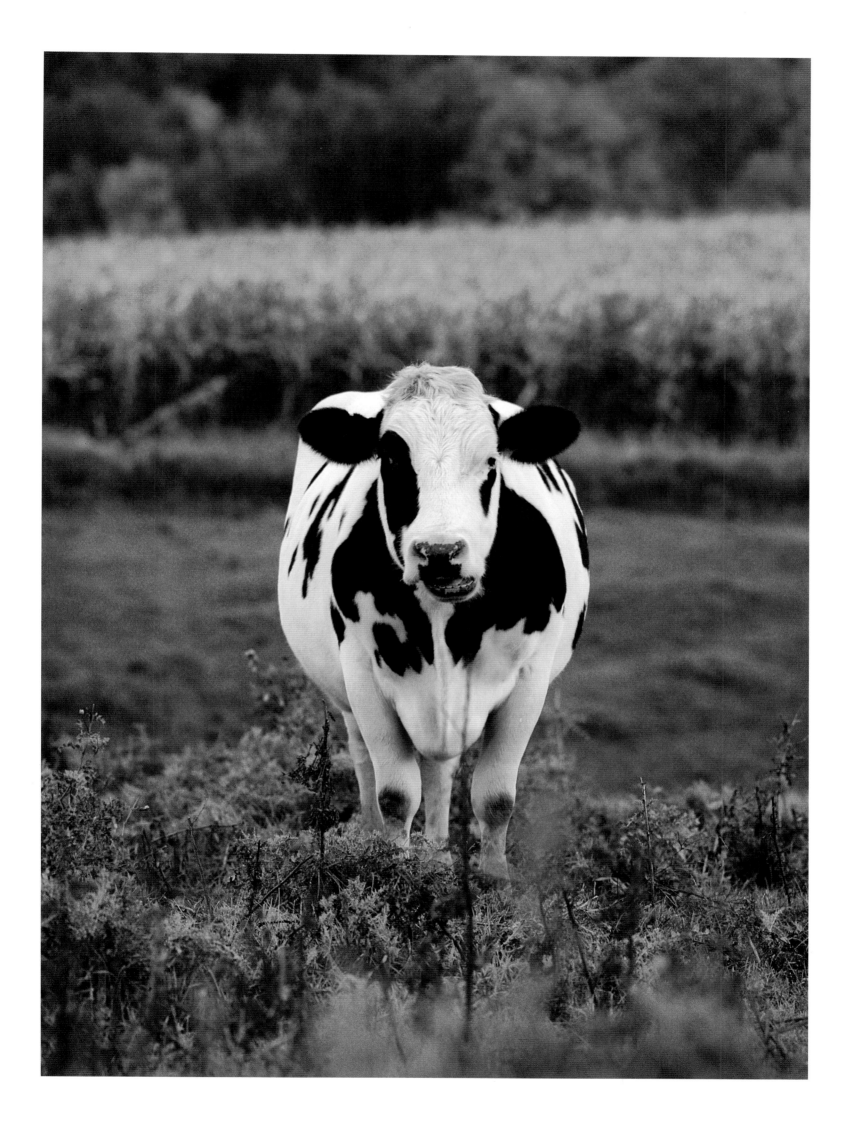

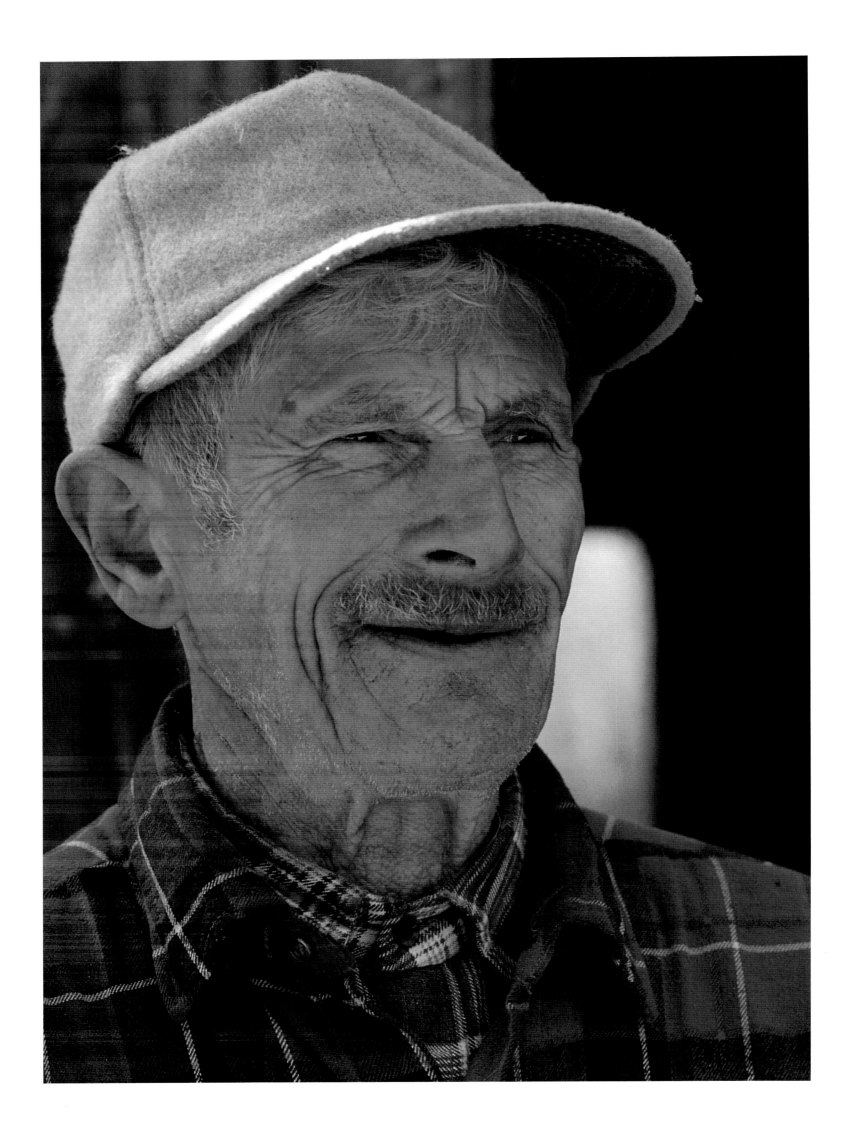

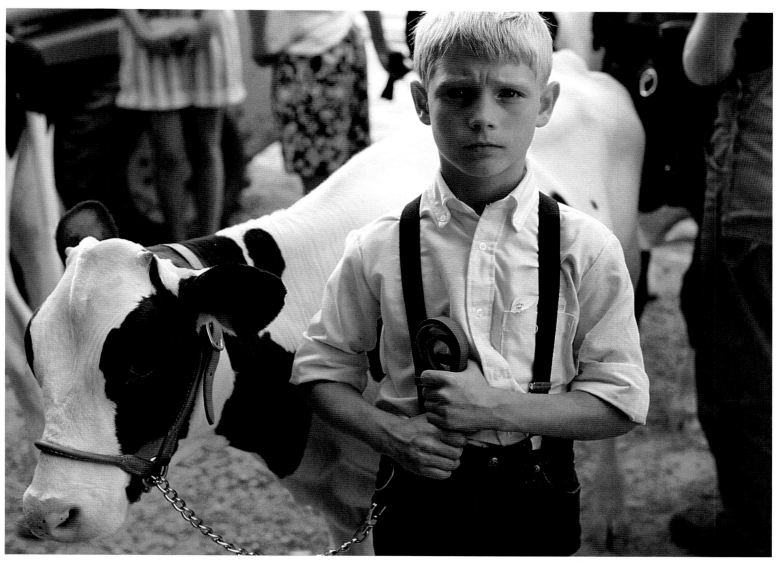

◄ A diversity of ethnic backgrounds has contributed to a varied, yet at the same time traditional, farm structure. Despite the nationwide growth of agribusiness, the small Wisconsin family farm is still able to function in ways unique to its background and experience.
▲ Stoughton, known as America's Little Norway, has maintained itself as a center of Norwegian heritage since the mid-nineteenth century. The annual Stoughton County Fair is one of more than seventy county fairs that occur each year around the state.

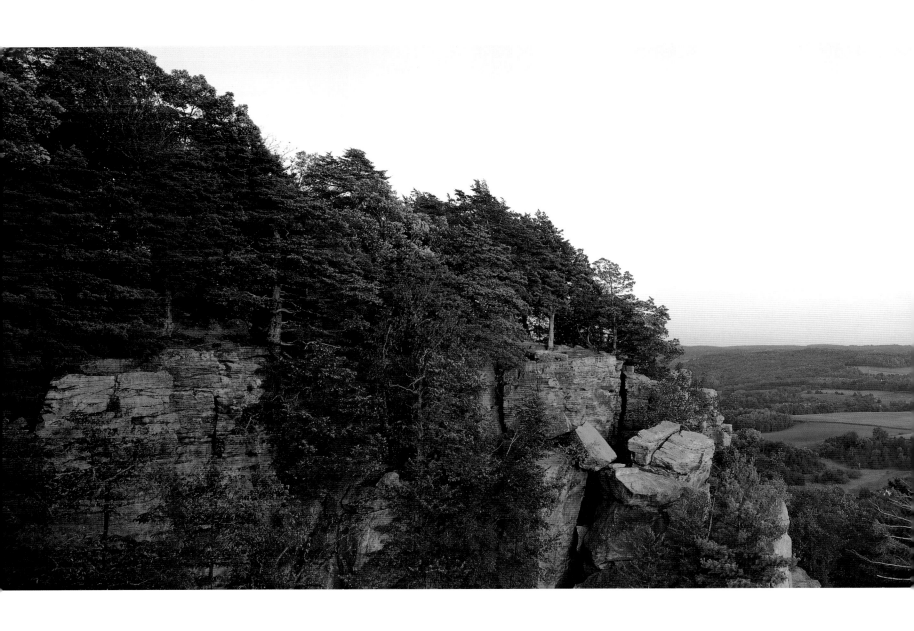

I climbed here at twilight to have an adventure, to look down on the homestead below as the bobcat watched the first settlers.

AUGUST DERLETH

Columbia County farmland from the Rocks of Gibraltar

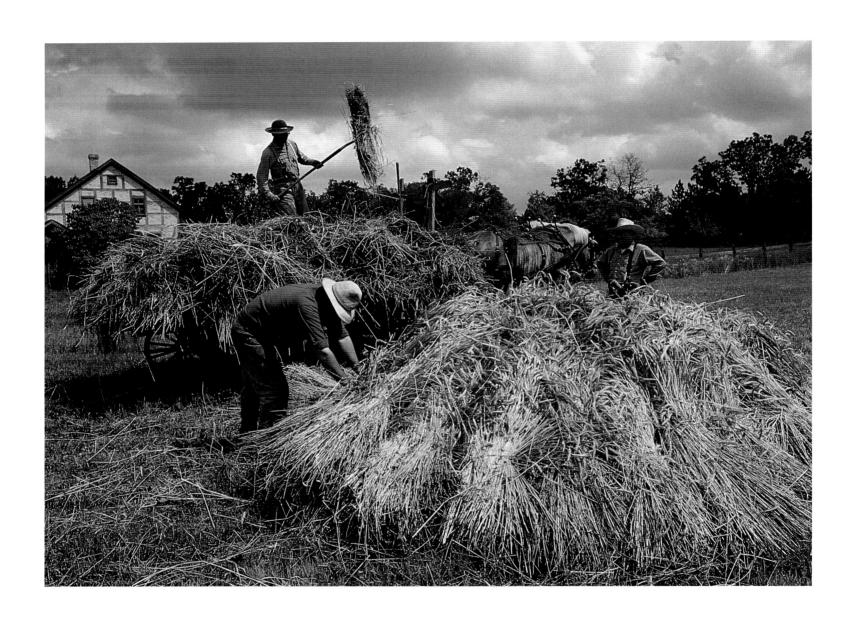

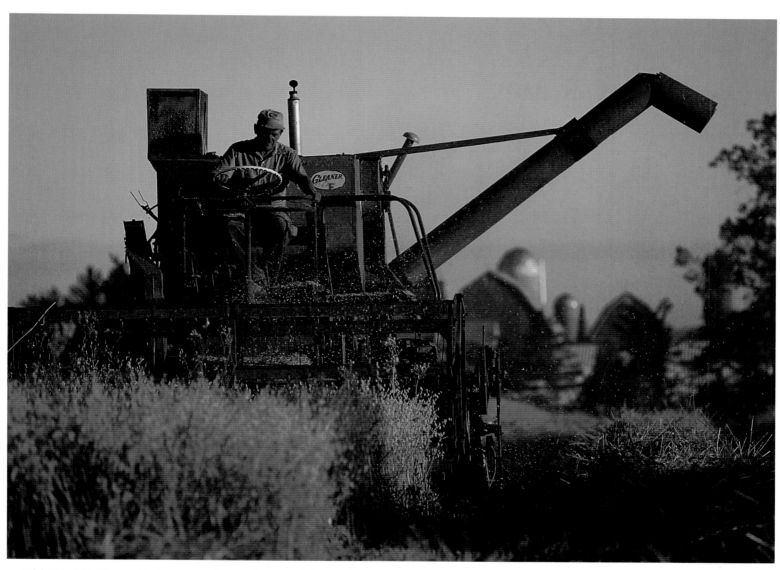

◄ Old World Wisconsin is an outdoor ethnic and living history museum occupying more than five hundred acres in the Kettle Moraine near Eagle. Visitors are able to experience ancestral life by watching authentically dressed and trained guides perform the daily chores that would have occurred throughout the seasons.
▲ Modern agribusiness is a key sector of Wisconsin's economy — with 85 percent of its food production shipped out of state. More acreage in Wisconsin is devoted to the growing of vegetables for processing than in any other state.

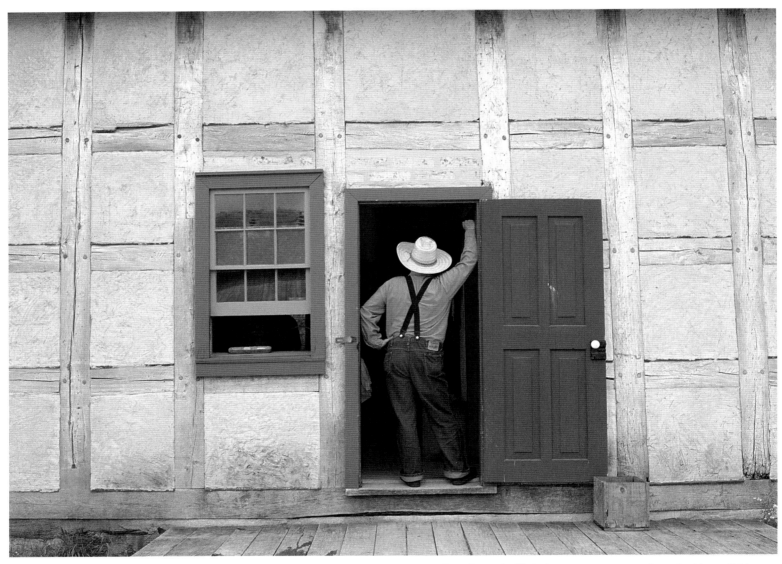

▲ Rare elsewhere, half-timber structures, such as the Koepsil House in the reconstructed German enclave at Old World Wisconsin, were a remarkable expression of an ancient European building tradition. ► The history of farming and the dignity of hard work are etched in the hands of Wisconsin farmers.

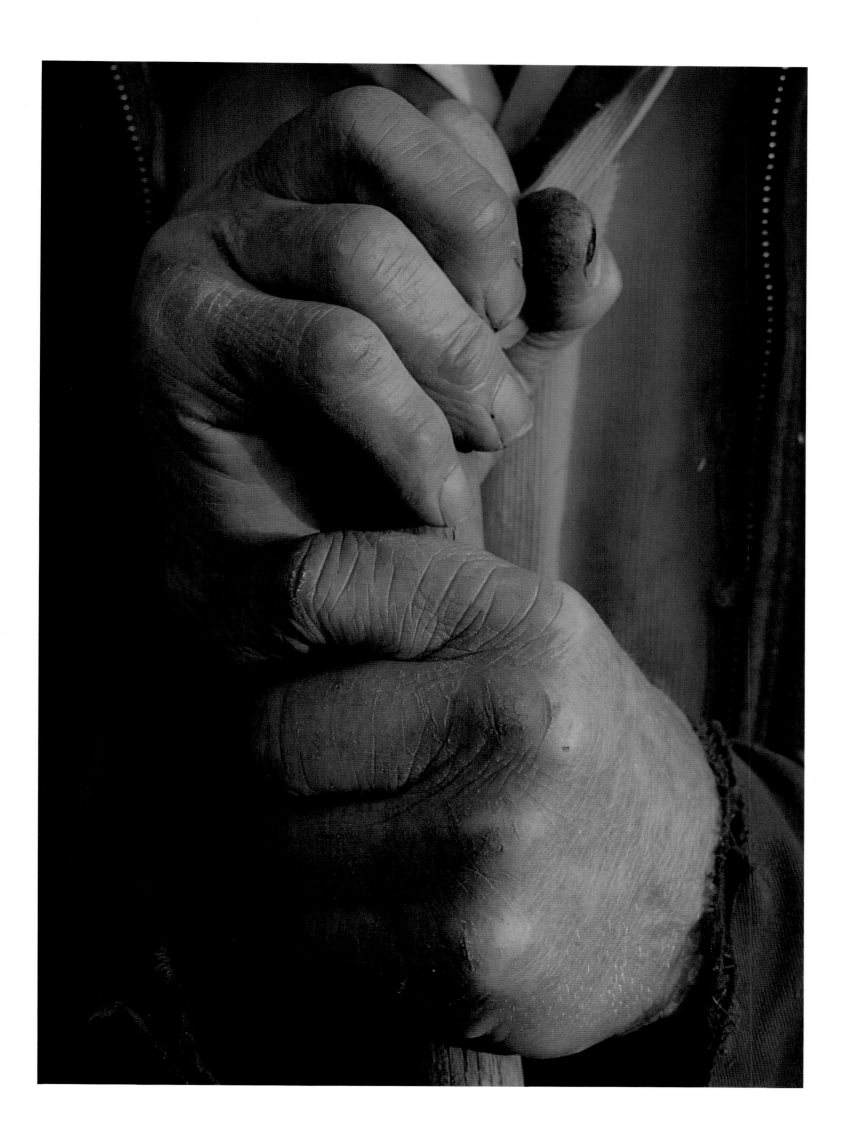

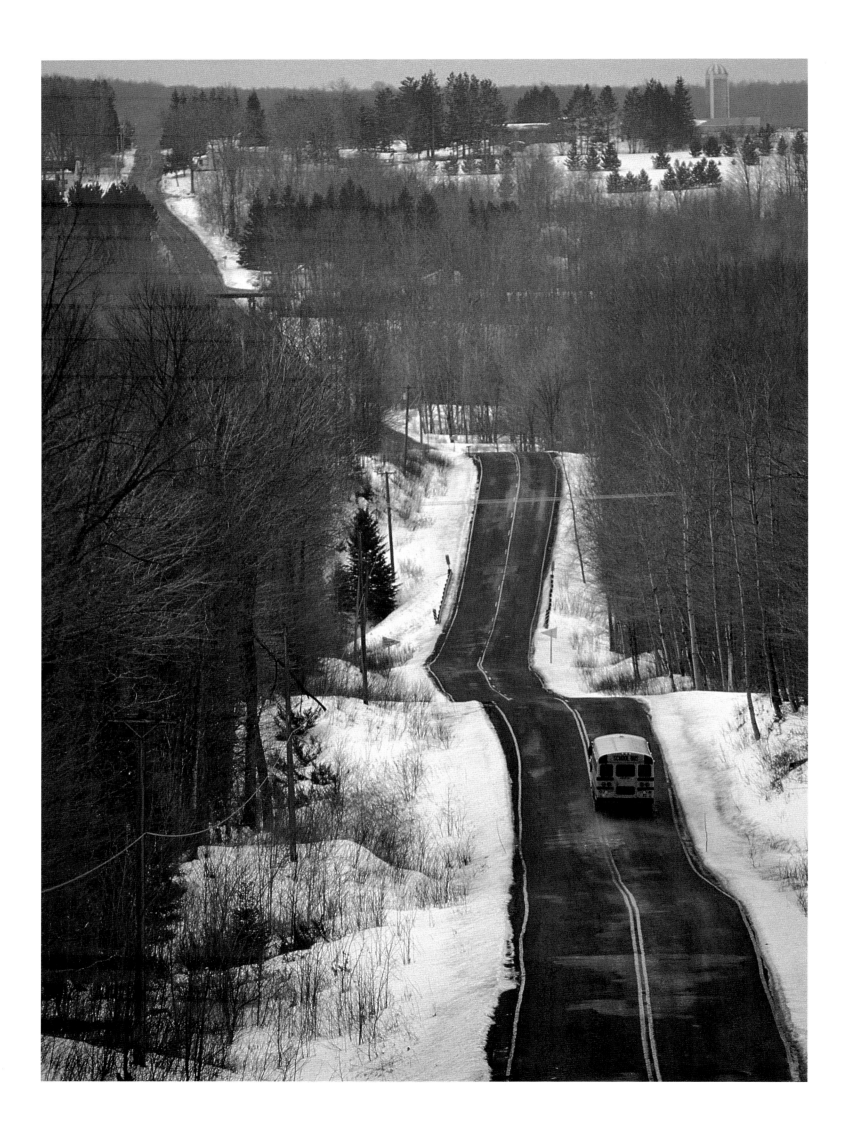

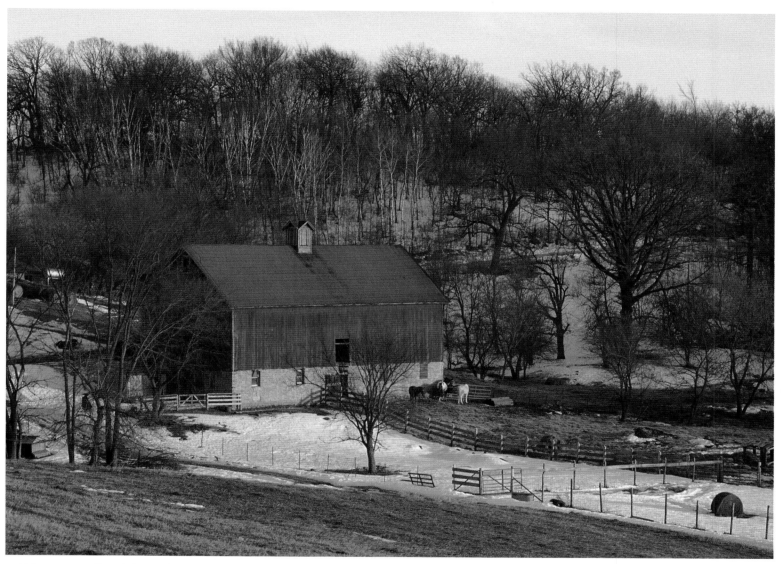

◄ Wisconsin offered free education in 1845, when its first public elementary school opened. In 1856, the first kindergarten in the nation was set up in Watertown, in northern Jefferson County.

▲ In 1870, most Wisconsin farmers grew wheat, a chancy crop that was hard on the soil. Newly arriving Scandinavian, German, and Swiss farmers turned to dairy farming, with which they were already familiar. Today, eight out of ten Wisconsin farmers are dairy farmers.

► ► July is Wisconsin's warmest month, with temperatures at times reaching 100°. Weather systems are slow moving, resulting in highly variable precipitation and storm patterns.

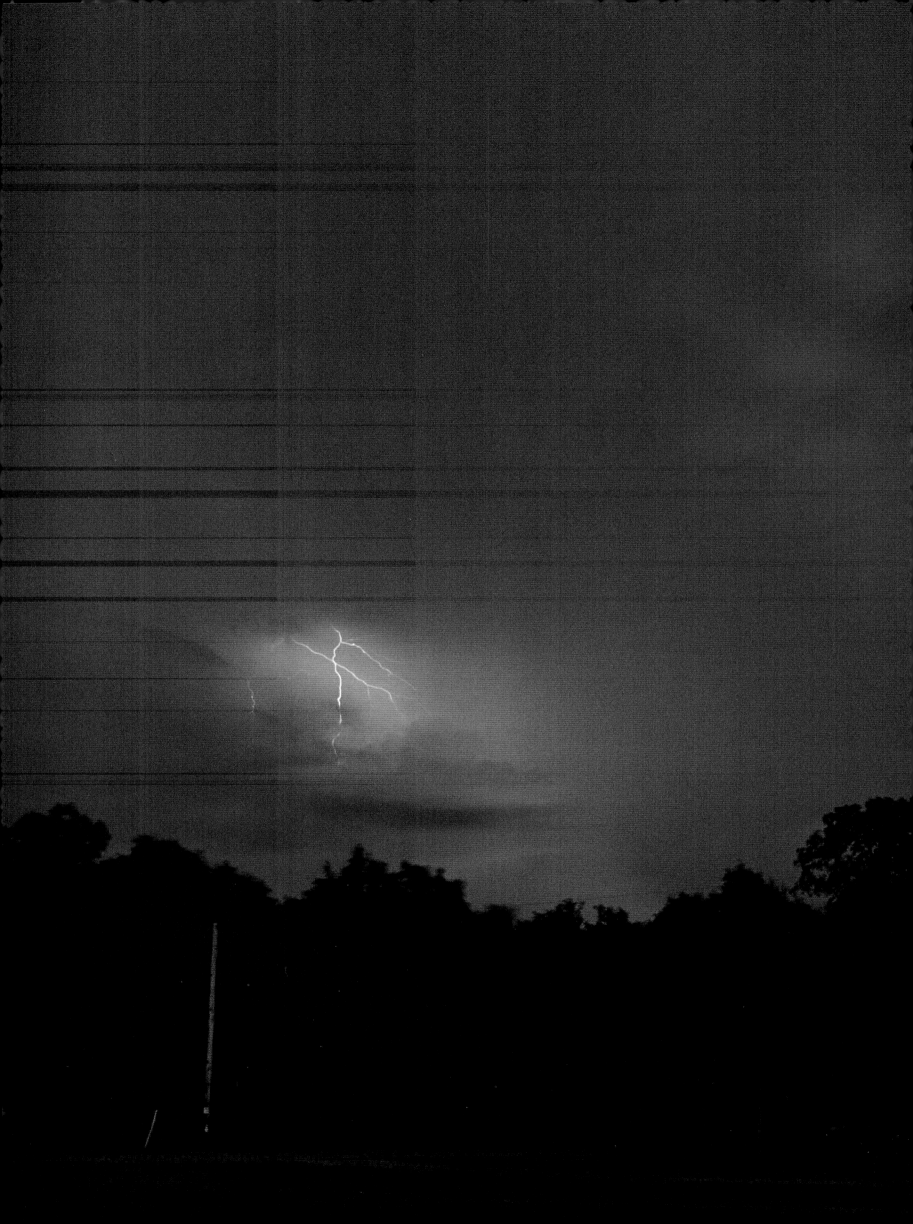

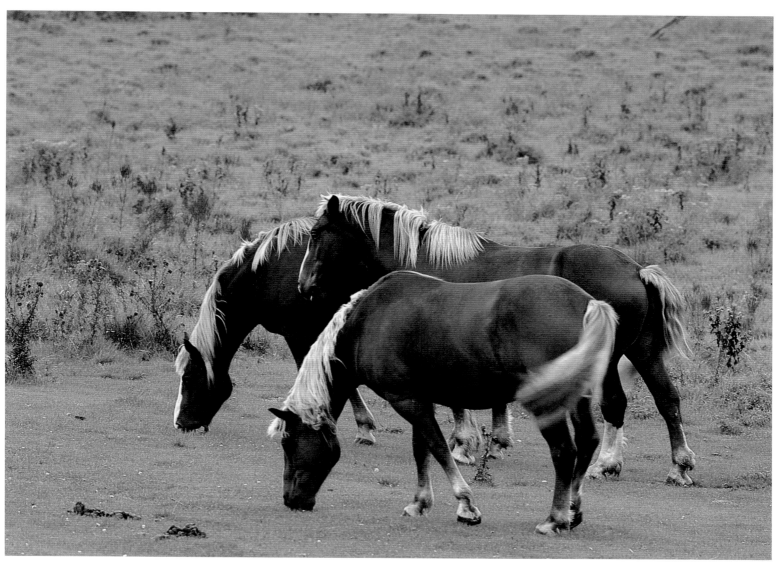

◄ An alternative type of dairy enterprise in the state is the production of goat's milk and goat cheese. A high-priced market, dairy goats are a viable operation for small-scale farms. Mohair from angora goats, used by fiber artists and in yarns for garments, is another niche market realized by a handful of Wisconsin suppliers.

▲ The introduction of Amish communities into Wisconsin is a recent development. Scattered in small pockets from New Glarus north to Augusta, the Amish continue to maintain a nonmechanized lifestyle utilizing horses for both labor and travel.

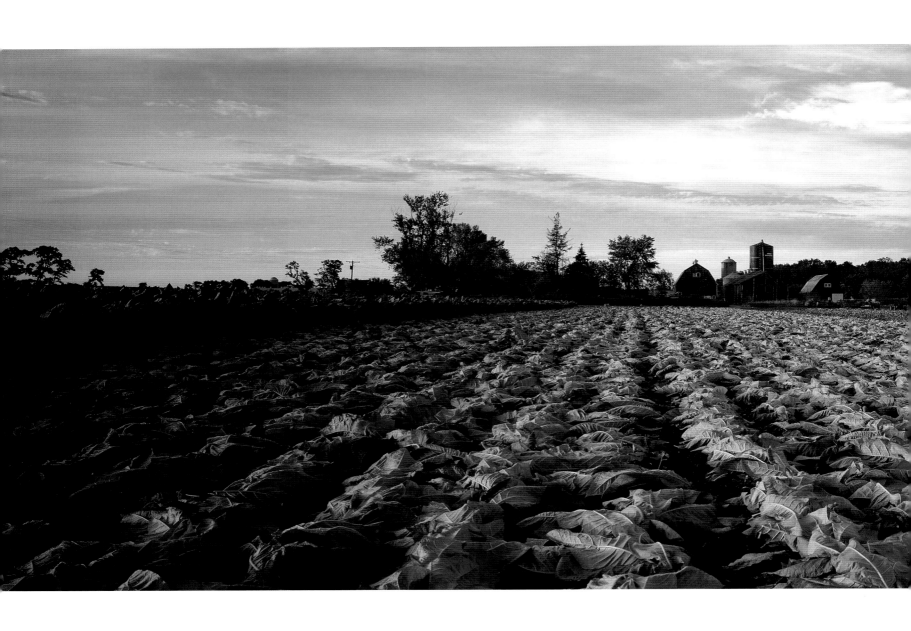

*The tobacco harvest, wading into
the green and cutting by hand,
generation after generation.*

ROBERT E. GARD

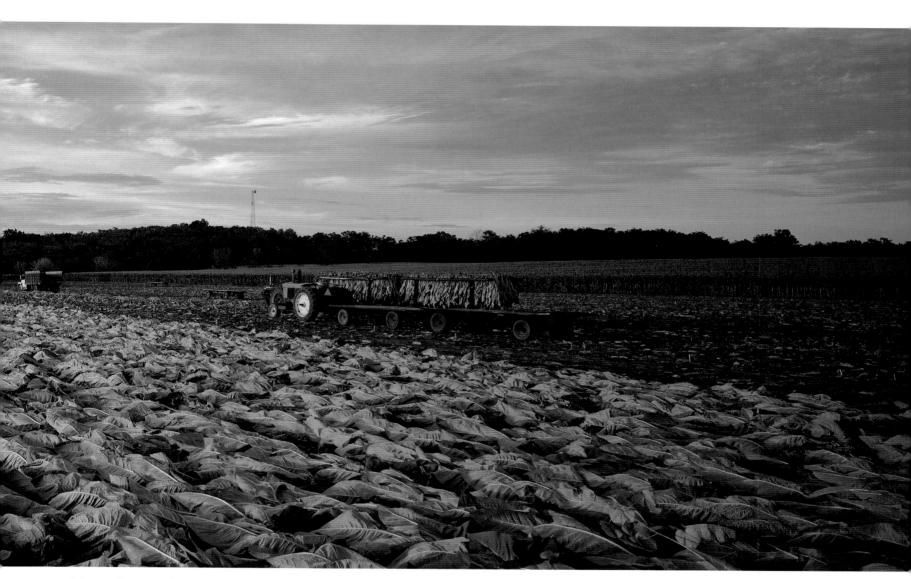

Tobacco harvest, Dane County

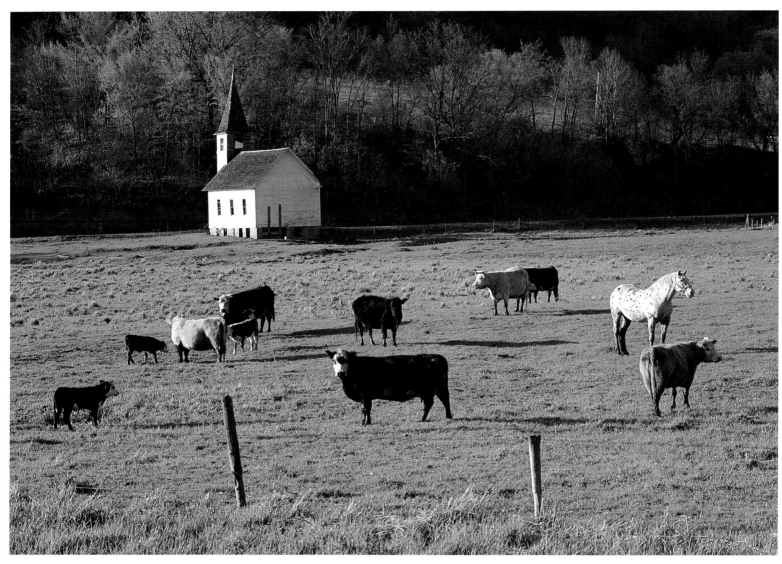

▲ The countryside around Barnum in Crawford County lies in the heart of the Driftless Area, a place unique in North America, for it gives us an idea of what the Middle West may have looked like before the Ice Age. It is endowed with angular rock formations, rolling wooded hillsides, and small lush valleys—all because it was never ground flat by the weight of the mile-high ice sheet.
► The city of Berlin in Green Lake County is architecturally rich in well-preserved, well-cared-for Victorian houses. Its early settlers arrived from New York and New England, bringing with them a taste for the best in prevailing architectural styles of the period.

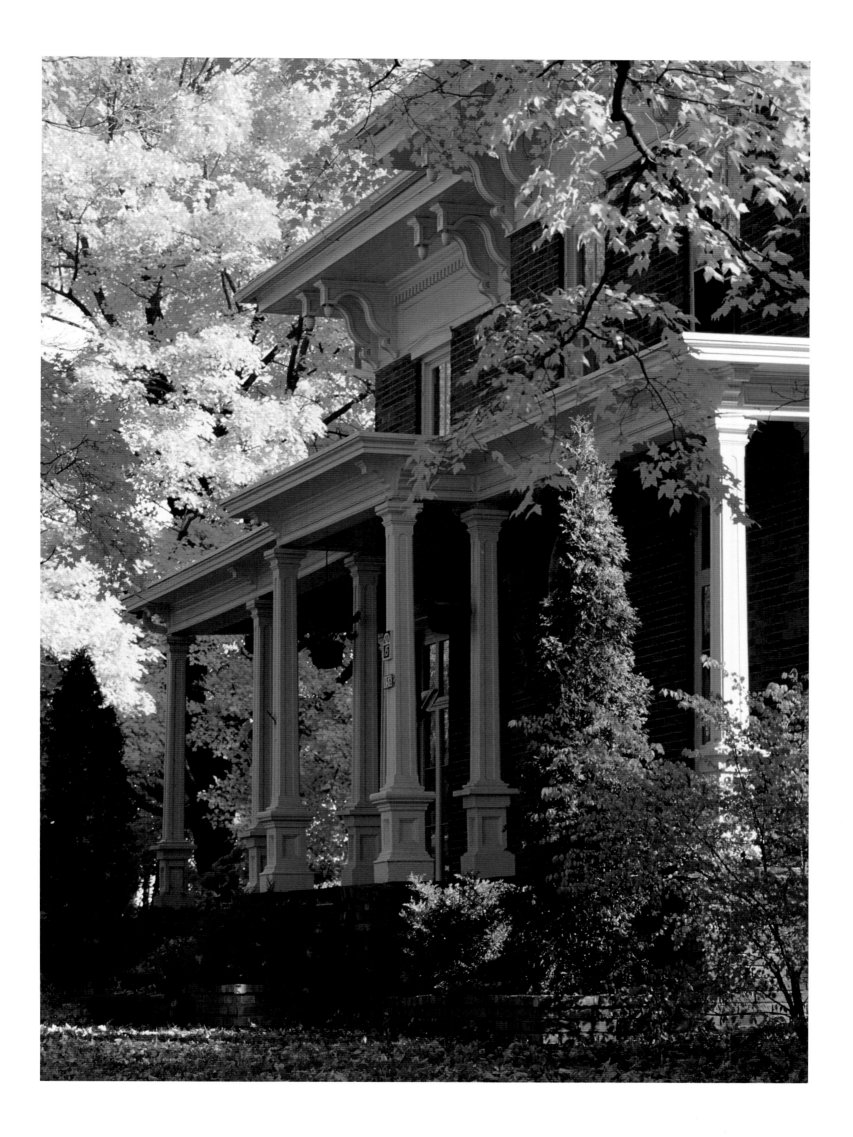

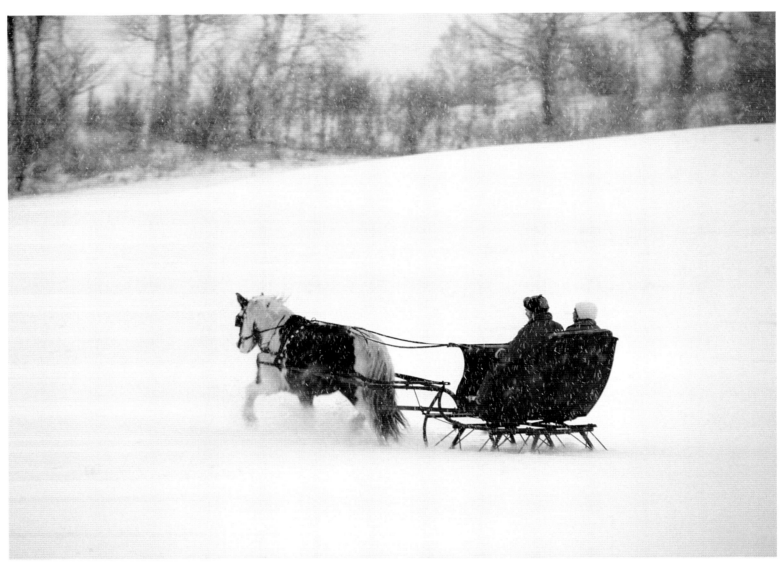

▲ Snowfall in the southern half of the state averages forty inches annually; in the northern snow-belt, ninety inches is not unusual, creating a wonderland for winter sports and recreational activities.
► The Mid-Continent Railway has been operating steam trains since 1963 and is dedicated to preserving turn-of-the-century steam equipment. The railway also houses an extensive collection of wooden passenger and freight cars.

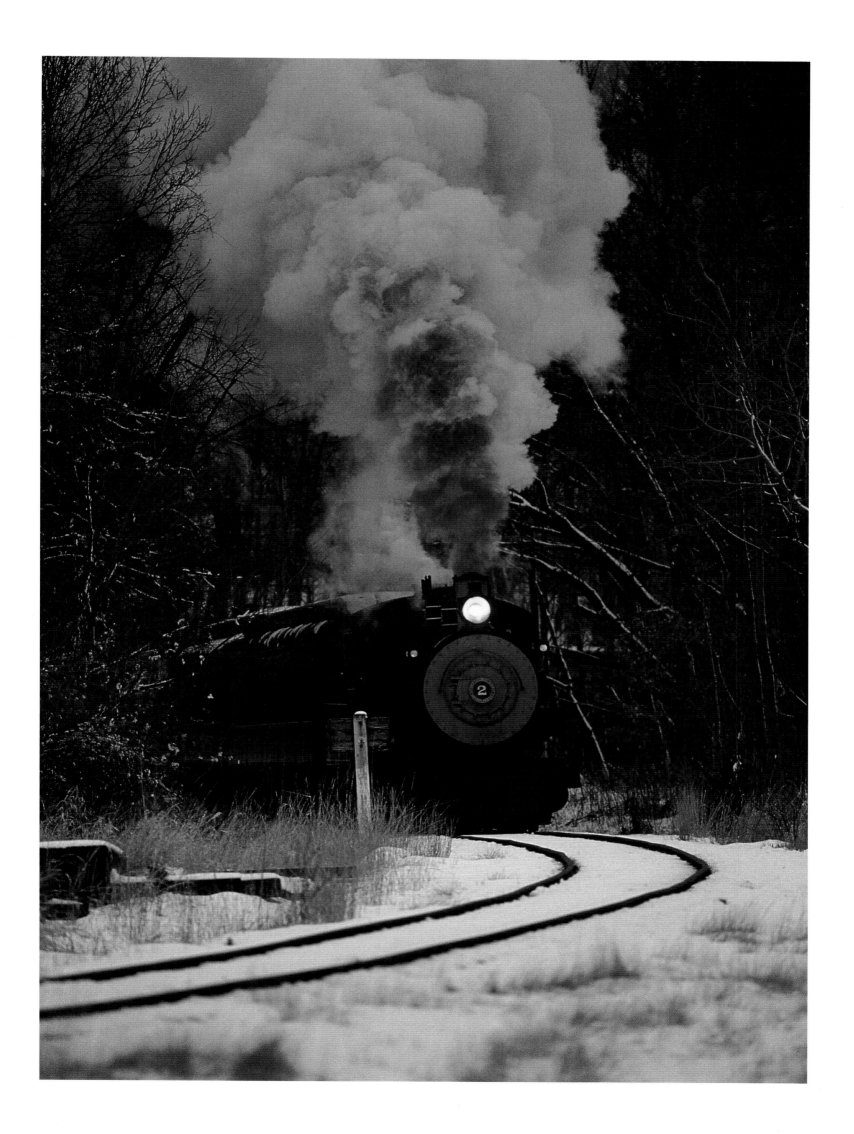

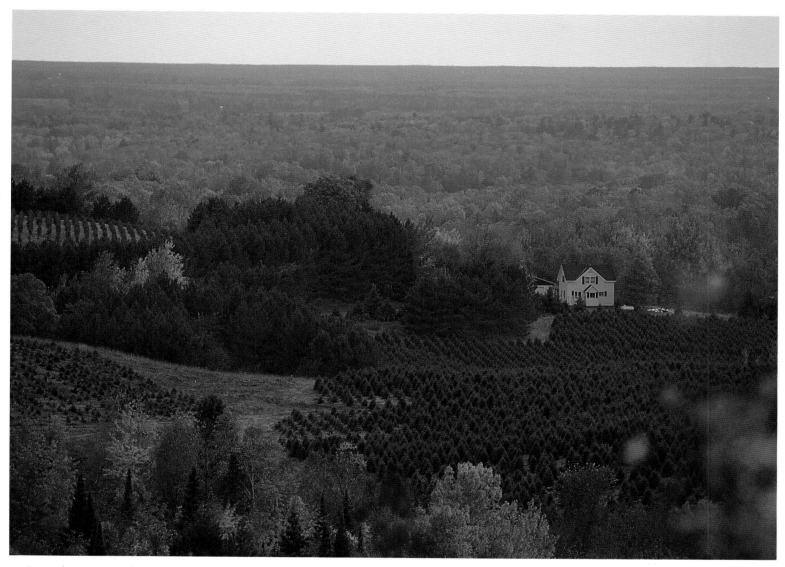

◄ Once known as Shantytown, Green Bay is Wisconsin's oldest settlement and is rich in historic buildings, including the state's oldest existing house, built in 1776, and Wisconsin's first courthouse. More than twenty-five historic structures are preserved at the forty-acre Heritage Hill State Park overlooking the Fox River. From these banks, the spread of civilization in Wisconsin began.
▲ Timm's Hill, near Ogema in Price County, is the true highest point in the state. At just under two thousand feet, it provides spectacular 180° views of the northern wooded countryside.

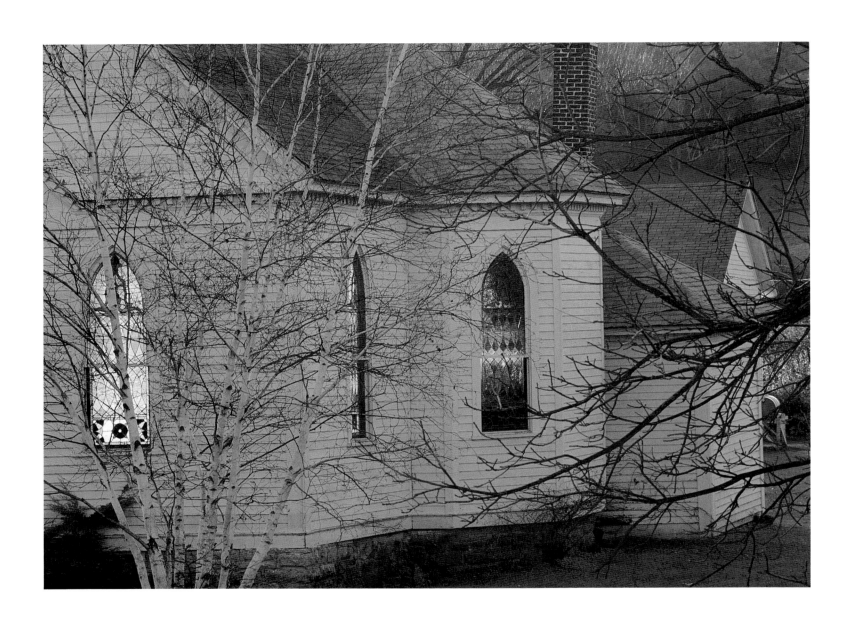

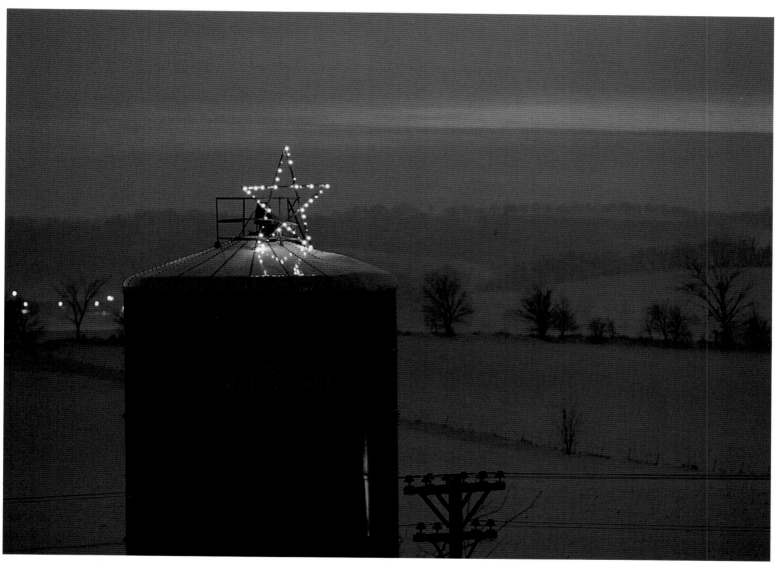

◄ White clapboard Protestant churches dot rural Wisconsin, giving some idea of the ethnic backgrounds of the area's inhabitants.
▲ During the Vietnam War years, Wisconsin farmers decorated their silos as beacons to those family members away from home. This symbol of homecoming lives on today.

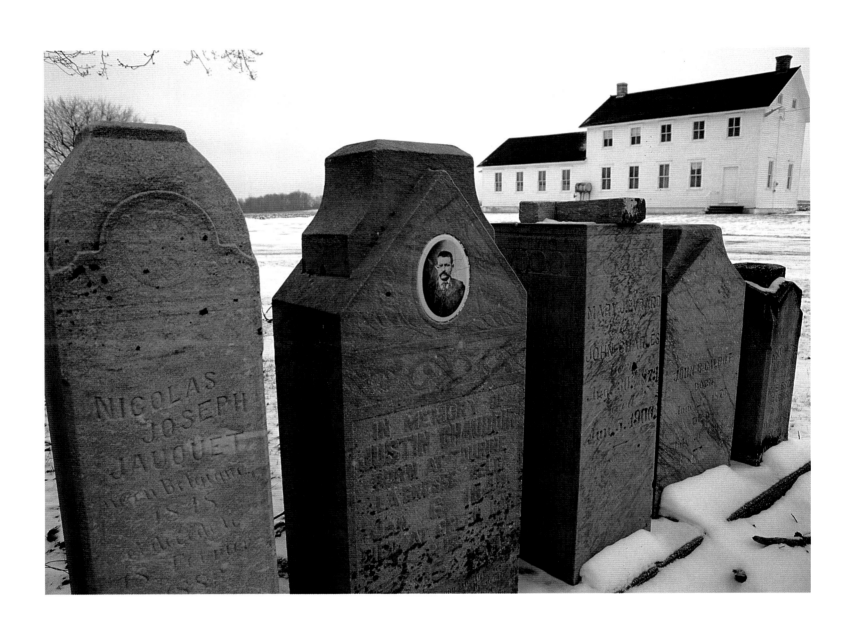

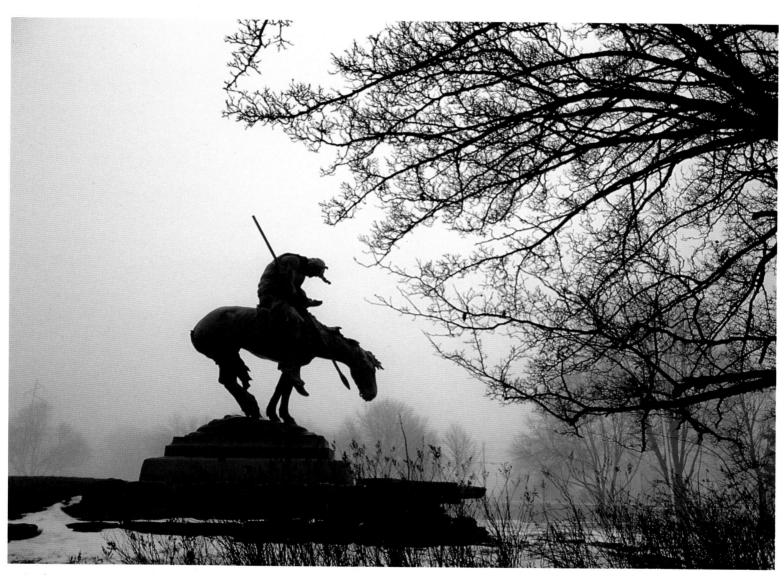

◄ At the convergence of Door, Kewaunee, and Brown counties, not far from Green Bay, Belgian immigrants acquired land that remains home to a homogenous ethnic settlement to this day.
▲ After appearing originally at the Panama Pacific Exposition in San Francisco in 1915, an original bronze casting of James Fraser's sculpture of Senneca chief Johnny Big Tree was commissioned by Waupun industrialist Clarence Shaler. It was presented to the city in 1929 and is called "The End of the Trail."

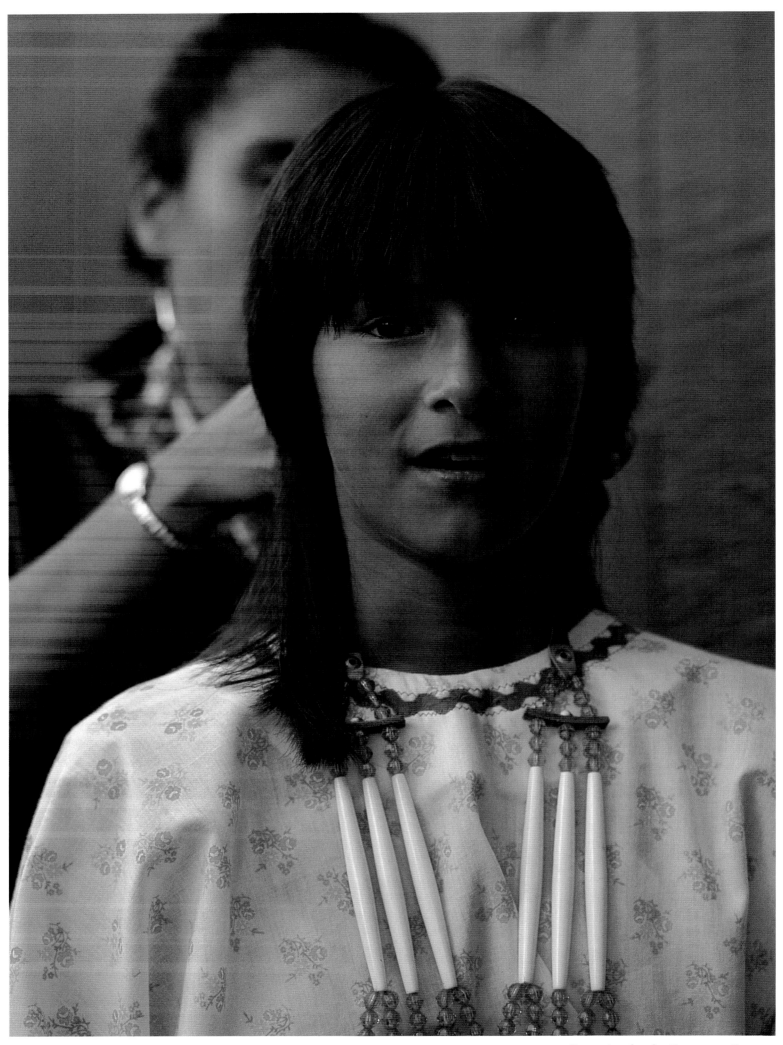

Preparing for the Pow-wow, Reserve

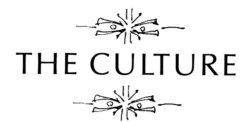

THE CULTURE

INDIAN CULTURE. Despite the best efforts of the Europeans to assimilate Native Americans into white culture—starting with the seventeenth-century Jesuits and continuing for more than three hundred years—the Native Americans of Wisconsin have proudly maintained their identity, character, and culture. Granted, significant accommodation has been made to the dominant white culture. Many of the old ways have been changed, and some have been forgotten, but the Indian culture is still strong in Wisconsin, and seemingly growing stronger each year.

When Wisconsin became a state, in 1848, the Native American population had been reduced to around ten thousand defeated, disorganized, and largely dispirited individuals. With the Indian way of life utterly destroyed and many suffering from disease or alcoholism, popular opinion among whites was that the Indians would soon either be assimilated into the dominant society or they would disappear altogether.

This has not happened. With improving health conditions and some federal protection, the state's Native American population has increased, from a low of 8,372 in the 1900 census, to 37,769 in the 1990 census. Active tribal societies, or nations, now include the Bad River, Lac Courte Oreilles, Lac du Flambeau, Menominee, Oneida, Potawatomi, Red Cliff, St. Croix, Sokaogon, Stockbridge-Munsee, and Winnebago. Most of these nations are located in northern Wisconsin, all away from urban areas.

Nearly half of Wisconsin's Indians today live on federally protected reservations, all in the north. Each reservation is governed by a tribal council, and its inhabitants are subject to some, but not all, state laws. Federal law, for instance, allows Indian gambling operations on reservation land, exempt from state gambling prohibitions. Tribes are also allowed special hunting and fishing privileges, guaranteed by nineteenth-century treaties in which Native Americans ceded their lands to the federal government. Both situations have drawn the opposition of some whites, who feel that their interests are being violated and challenged unfairly. In recent years, the growth in gambling operations—from crude bingo halls to Las Vegas-like casinos—has brought some tribes out of general poverty for the first time in recent history.

Wisconsin Native Americans today depend greatly on tourist dollars. Some reservations have large motels and restaurants, as well as bars, sporting goods stores, and souvenir shops selling everything from locally made moccasins and exquisite baskets to rubber hatchets imported from Asian countries.

There are also successful Indian-owned businesses situated off the reservations. One prime example is the Winnebago Public Indian Museum, four miles north of Wisconsin Dells, Wisconsin's most popular tourist area. The museum, owned and run by the Little Eagle family, displays Indian artifacts, beadwork, feather head dresses and other items, and an adjoining gift shop sells Native American crafts. Locally made Winnebago baskets are a popular item, as well as deerskin moccasins, silver jewelry, and Navaho blankets. The operation started as a small Indian basket stand on the highway and grew over the years into a major retail operation.

Visitors to the Wisconsin Dells have been going to the Stand Rock Indian Ceremonial since 1929, making it the longest-running attraction in the area. The show combines Indian lore, costumes, and dances, all performed in a natural rock amphitheater on the banks of the Wisconsin River. The Kickapoo Indian Caverns, in

Wauzeka, are the largest cave system in the state. The caverns were long used by local Indian tribes, then they were mined by early settlers, and now they have become a prime tourist site.

Wisconsin tribes are also sponsoring summer events to entertain tourists and to teach them more about the Wisconsin Indian way of life. A powwow contest is held in early June in Hayward, sponsored by the Lac Courte Oreilles Ojibwa School. Ojibwa Craft Days are held in late June on Madeline Island. An "Honor the Earth" powwow, sponsored by many tribes, is held in July, in Hayward. Other powwows are held in Odanah and Webster in late August, to coincide with the wild rice harvest.

Today, Wisconsin's Indian peoples, although not yet out of the poverty that has plagued them since the earliest days of westward expansion, are facing the future with guarded optimism. Their culture and way of life are respected by the white community as never before (especially as whites begin to question their own relationship to the environment), their businesses are flourishing, their health care improving, their population growing, and their relations with white governments improving. The Indian peoples will be a viable force in Wisconsin for the foreseeable future.

RICH ETHNIC DIVERSITY. Wisconsin, the promised land for so many European immigrants a century or more ago, has inherited a rich cultural legacy from this mix of peoples. The names of the towns alone—New Glarus, New London, New Berlin, New Lisbon, New Rome, New Amsterdam, New Munster—attest to the diversity and to the hope these people brought with them. These immigrants were proud of their heritage, but also determined to start life anew, in a new land of opportunity.

The French, of course, were the first immigrants to arrive, but they came mostly to trade in furs or to convert the savages to Christianity, and they left little behind and had little real lasting influence. The entire Great Lakes region was claimed for King Louis XIV of France, in 1671, but the British seized control by 1763 and many of the French retreated into Canada. Since 1800, those French who have migrated into Wisconsin have come through Canada. Few French have ever migrated into Wisconsin from France itself. By 1940, there were some twenty-two thousand people of French descent living in the state, some in communities with French names, such as Marinette, Fond du Lac, and Prairie du Chien. Wisconsin's most famous citizen of French descent is undoubtedly Robert "Fighting Bob" La Follette, the leader of the Progressive Republicans in the early part of the twentieth century, United States Senator, and presidential candidate.

The British were first to settle in significant numbers, but many of them came "once removed," migrating here from New York and Vermont. Cornish miners flocked to southwest Wisconsin in the 1830s to work the lead mines. The Welsh brought expertise in stock breeding, and the Scotch brought a taste for hard work and frugality. Their most famous immigrant son was John Muir, who became father of the national park system, founder of the Sierra Club, and America's greatest environmentalist.

The German immigration began in 1840 and lasted into the early 1900s. In the decade between 1844 and 1854, more than a million Germans came to America, many settling in Wisconsin, which still had prime farmland to offer. By 1900, Wisconsin had more than 268,000 German-born residents. Milwaukee became the most "German" city in Wisconsin. The Germans were hard workers and good farmers. They also had a rich musical heritage and brought a keen knowledge of beer brewing, for which Milwaukee is still famous.

The Norwegians were happy to settle in Wisconsin. They were one immigrant group to leave behind colder winters than they found in Wisconsin. They were also happy to find that farmland was far more productive and easier to work than the stony soils of the old country, and taxes here were considerably lower. The Norwegian migration began as early as 1838, but reached a peak at the turn of the century. More than twenty-four thousand Norwegians immigrated to American in 1903, and many found new homes in Wisconsin and Minnesota. Today, the Norwegian heritage is kept alive through celebrations such as Syttende Mai (Norwegian Independence Day) in communities such as Westby and Stoughton. Norwegian pioneer days are reenacted at Little Norway and at Old World Wisconsin, two living museums.

Between 1900 and 1910, more than fifty-eight thousand Finns came to America. Like other Scandinavian immigrants, they found Wisconsin to be quite hospitable. The lakes and pine forests reminded them of home, and, once again, the farmland here was plentiful, productive, and cheap. The communities in the northern part of the state, such as Oulu and Oma, are reminders of the Finnish influence in Wisconsin.

The Dutch were early migrants to America, many coming because of the potato failure of 1845-46. Others came because of religious differences with the Reformed Church. Centers of Dutch settlement were Milwaukee, Alto (Fond du Lac County), Oostburg and Cedar Grove (Sheboygan County), Little Chute (Outagamie County), Holland (Brown County), and New Amsterdam. The biggest Dutch celebration today is the Holland Festival, held the last weekend in July at Cedar Grove. Dutch foods are served, Klompan Dancers clomp around in wooden shoes, and Main Street is scrubbed down with brooms and brushes in preparation for the big parade.

The potato failure that spurred Dutch migration was far worse in Ireland, where it led to true famine. In 1846, the Irish potato crop was a total failure, and was followed by an especially cold winter. Hundreds of thousands of poor and hungry Irish came streaming to America. By 1850, there were more than twenty-one thousand Irish in Wisconsin, nearly five thousand of them living in Milwaukee. Today, descendants of the Irish immigrants live in every part of the state, emerging every St. Patrick's day to celebrate the Emerald Isle.

Swiss immigration was never very heavy in Wisconsin, but those Swiss who did come brought invaluable knowledge: they knew how to make Swiss cheese. One hundred thirty-eight Swiss emigrated from Glarus canton to Green County, Wisconsin, in 1845. They built Swiss-style thatched cottages, shared all mineral wealth and other natural resources, and set about to prosper in the New World. New Glarus is still a very Swiss community today. The old German dialect is still spoken, and the town celebrates its rich European heritage at every opportunity.

The center of Polish migration in Wisconsin was in Portage County, around Stevens Point. Others settled in Trempealeau

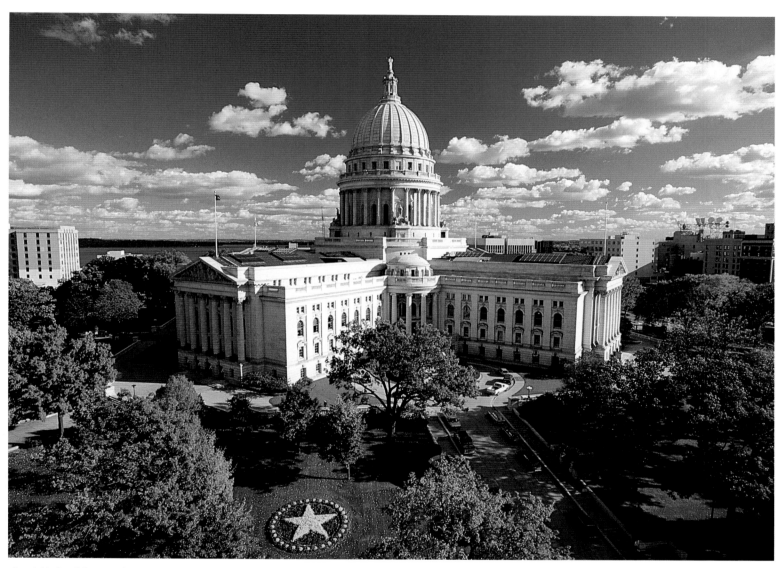

The fifth building to house Wisconsin's state government—the third in Madison—was completed in 1917. Designed in the form of a Greek cross, the central white dome is crowned by "Wisconsin," the fifteen-foot gold-leaf statue by sculptor Daniel Chester French.

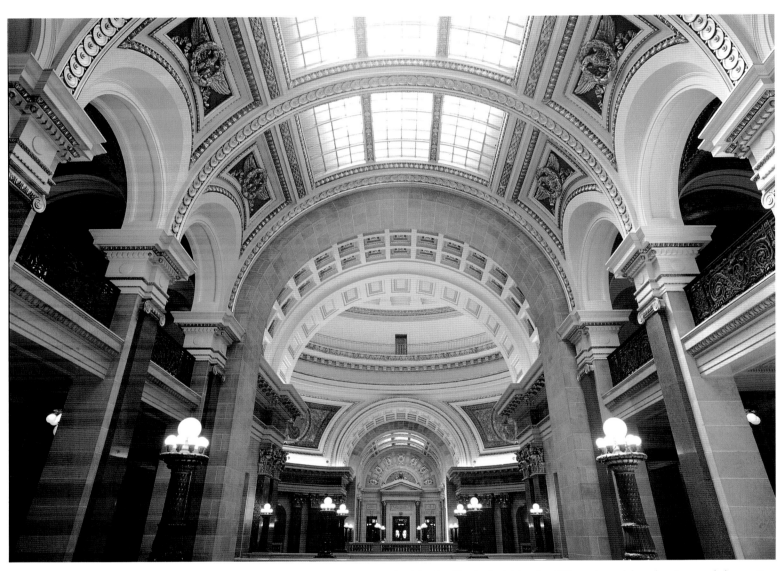

Inside the Capitol, thirty-six different marbles, foreign and domestic, were used to help construct the many chambers, arches, passageways, and sweeping staircases — all of which lead to the stately central rotunda, crowned by the decorated dome 250 feet above.

County or near Green Bay. Because they arrived relatively late, the Polish immigrants had to buy "cutover land," fields of pine stumps that the loggers had left behind, or farms that other Americans had abandoned because they were too difficult to work. Another group of Polish immigrants from Upper Silesia settled in Trempealeau County in 1862. By 1880, there were 165 Silesian families in Trempealeau County. By 1910, one out of every three people in Portage County was of Polish descent. And by 1920, there were about ninety thousand Poles living in Milwaukee.

Hispanic migration to Wisconsin has been a recent event. Puerto Ricans began to move to Milwaukee after World War II, to work in the factories there. The Puerto Rican population of the city jumped from about three hundred in 1950 to nearly thirteen thousand by 1980. Mexicans were also drawn to factory jobs in Milwaukee, while others came as migrant workers and stayed on permanently. When Congress restricted European immigration in 1917, Wisconsin sugar beet farmers called on Mexican-American workers from Texas to help harvest the crop. The Hispanic community in Wisconsin today, although still small, is a spirited one, with celebrations and festivals held in Milwaukee and other cities each Mexican Independence Day.

WHAT WISCONSINITES DO. Although Wisconsin has its share of museums, art galleries, symphony orchestras, live theater, and other indoor cultural attractions, residents are primarily outdoor-oriented. And although Wisconsin supports major league teams in baseball, football, and basketball, the residents are far more apt to be playing softball than watching a major league baseball game, more likely to be snowmobiling or cross-country skiing than watching a professional hockey game. Wisconsinites travel to Chicago or Minneapolis for the best in theater. Chicago and Minneapolis residents come to Wisconsin for the best in fishing and camping.

From dipping a line off a northwoods pier for panfish, to fishing through the ice for winter lake perch, to trolling for giant coho salmon in Lake Michigan, Wisconsin is a fisherman's paradise. There are more than 160 trout streams and hundreds of lakes stocked with muskellunge, northern and walleye pike, large- and smallmouth bass, and a variety of panfish. For big-water action, Lakes Superior and Michigan offer chink and coho salmon, and big brown, rainbow, and lake trout.

Although outdoorsmen also go for rabbits, squirrels, grouse, pheasant, quail, woodcock, and wild turkeys, the major hunting action centers on the white-tailed deer. Wisconsin, situated on the populous Mississippi Flyway, also offers fine waterfowl gunning every autumn. With more than seventy state parks, forests, trails, and recreation areas, Wisconsin has great routes for bicycling, hiking, and cross-country skiing. Often, the same trails are used for all three, and some allow snowmobiling, as well. The Elroy-Sparta Trail, lying along thirty-two miles of abandoned railroad bed, includes three tunnels. The Ice Age Trail, a National Scenic Trail, follows the leading edge of the last glacier, and will cover a thousand miles when it is completed.

More than thirty-five state parks offer camping. The largest, Peninsula State Park, in popular Door County, has 467 sites. Devil's Lake State Park, the most heavily visited, follows with 459.

But there are also some parks with many more raccoons and white-tailed deer than people, where campers can really get away from the crowds and urban stress. The state parks, exceptionally well maintained, range from the rustic to the semiluxurious in their amenities. Some have electric outlets, flush toilets, showers, concession stands, water skiing, and handicap facilities. Most have nature, hiking, skiing, and snowmobile trails, and facilities for picnicking, swimming, canoeing, motorboating, and fishing. Scores of private campgrounds offer swimming pools, tennis courts, family entertainment centers, RV hookups, telephones, even cable TV for those who like to "rough it easy."

With thousands of miles of both quiet and rushing streams and rivers, Wisconsin is ideally fitted for some of the finest canoeing in the nation. A few of the more popular rivers are the Wisconsin, the Chippewa, which offers Class I-III rapids, and the scenic Brule, which follows the border between Wisconsin and Michigan through the Nicolet National Forest. The Apple River, near the Interstate State Park, is a popular stream for tubing, and is likely to be jammed with relaxed and happy tubers every weekend during daylight in July and August.

Tennis courts and golf courses, both public and private, are ubiquitous in the state. There are twenty downhill ski areas, featuring runs as long as 5,300 feet. Granted, Wisconsin is no Snowbird or Vail—the glaciers saw to that—but there is still plenty of winter fun to be had on these more modest slopes.

Farmers' markets are fun and popular events for both residents and tourists. They are dotted through the state, but the largest is in Madison, held every Saturday morning from spring through fall, and filling the eight-block sidewalk area around the State Capitol building.

Sports fans will not go hungry in Wisconsin. Major league teams here include the Milwaukee Brewers American League baseball team, with games played in Milwaukee County Stadium; the Green Bay Packers National Football League team, playing in Lambeau Field in Green Bay and in Milwaukee County Stadium; and the Milwaukee Bucks National Basketball Association team, which plays at the Bradley Center. Milwaukee also supports professional hockey and soccer teams, and even a professional polo club. The University of Wisconsin, at Madison, supplies most of the collegiate sports action, although the Marquette Warriors, in Milwaukee, have a rich basketball tradition.

Wisconsin is also home to Road America, the longest course on the Indycar circuit, and to many other speedways throughout the state. The Wisconsin Olympic Ice Rink is one of only three 400-meter, oval, refrigerated rinks in the nation, and is home training ground for the United States Olympic Speed Skating team.

Wisconsin also has its share of higher culture. The Milwaukee Symphony and Milwaukee Ballet give excellent performances throughout the year, for both adults and children. American Players Theater, near Spring Green, is recognized as one of the nation's finest Shakespearean companies. Classical concerts are presented during summer evenings on the grounds of the State Capitol building in Madison.

ATTRACTIONS AND EVENTS. There is never a lack of things to do or places to go in Wisconsin—there are only choices to be made. Major museums include the Milwaukee Public Museum, one of the largest and finest natural history museums in the nation, featuring a recreated Costa Rican rain forest and the popular "Streets of Old Milwaukee." Also renowned are the Milwaukee Art Museum; the Paine Art Center and Arboretum, in Oshkosh; the State Historical Museum, in Madison; and the Elvehjem Museum of the University of Wisconsin-Madison.

The Experimental Aircraft Association Museum, in Oshkosh, displays historic aircraft ranging from some of the smallest craft, to a World War I B-17 bomber, to a replica of the *Voyageur*. Old World Wisconsin, a living outdoor museum, near Eagle, demonstrates how immigrants lived and worked in the last century. Heritage Hill, near Green Bay, does much the same on a smaller scale.

The Green Bay Packer Hall of Fame, in Green Bay, has displays of interest to all football fans. The House on the Rock, near Spring Green, is perhaps the most popular single tourist attraction in the state, a giant and eclectic collection of objects ranging from automated music rooms, to fantastic doll houses, to the world's largest carousel. (Sorry—no rides on the carousel.) And the Manitowoc Maritime Museum, on the shore of Lake Michigan, has excellent displays of more than a century of Lake Michigan maritime history, including a genuine World War II submarine.

Wisconsin is the home of Frank Lloyd Wright and his famous Taliesin home and studio, near Spring Green. Public tours are given spring through fall. In Baraboo, a major attraction is Circus World Museum, a fifty-acre state historic site presenting circus acts, demonstrations, daily shows, and an outstanding exhibit of nineteenth-century circus wagons and equipment. Both kids and parents love it.

The Milwaukee County Zoo is one of the finest in the world. On the 184-acre grounds, animals are displayed in natural settings, without bars. The International Crane Foundation, near Baraboo, is an educational and research center offering public tours. Many cranes from around the world may be seen there.

Wisconsin has scores of educational nature centers. One of the best is the Wehr Nature Center, in Milwaukee. It has two hundred acres of restored prairie, woodland, and wetland areas, and a small lake. It is located in Witnall Park, near the outstanding Boerner Botanical Gardens. Other superb nature centers include the Schlitz Audubon Center, in Milwaukee; Bay Beach Wildlife Sanctuary, in Green Bay; and the Woodland Dunes Nature Center, north of Manitowoc.

FESTIVALS, FAIRS, AND CELEBRATIONS. Wisconsinites are wild about fairs and festivals. With intense competition among communities for tourist dollars, there is certainly a wide menu of events going on every weekend of the year, especially in the summer months.

Start with the biggest of the big—the Wisconsin State Fair. Held early each August, near Milwaukee, the State Fair offers something for everyone, including big-name entertainers, stock car races, thousands of prize farm animals, a huge midway, and plenty of food. Other annual events in Milwaukee include the big July Circus Parade, Summerfest, and ethnic festivals sponsored by the city's Italian, French, German, Afro-American, Irish, Mexican, Native American, and Greek communities. There is a big Holiday Folk Fair in November, and a Winterfest celebration in January and February.

Other annual events in the state range from fairly big to very small, hometown, and homespun efforts. The fun begins as early as March, with the Minocqua Spring Festival (celebrating the end of ski season), Muskie Magic in New London, and Maple Syrup Saturday in Appleton.

In April, the Little Britches Rodeo is held in Tomah; Boom With a View (referring to the mating rituals of prairie chickens) takes place in Amherst Junction; and the Norwegian Easter Festival occurs in Dodgeville.

In May, the festival season begins to heat up, with Wild Turkey Weekend in Boscobel, the Kite Fly in Oshkosh, wildflower tours in a number of communities, Old Peninsula Days in Fish Creek, Syttende Mai (Norwegian Independence Day) in Westby and Stoughton, Swiss Polkafest in New Glarus, the Amish Quilt Auction in Amherst, Sunfish Days in Onalaska, and the Apple Blossom Festival in Gays Mills.

June is National Dairy Month, and so there are Dairy Days in West Salem, Butterfest in Sparta, Butter Fest in Reedsburg, and the Great Wisconsin Cheese Festival in Little Chute. Dairy cows are brought to downtown Madison for the Cows on the Concourse celebration. June is also Frank Lloyd Wright's birthday, and so he is feted in his home town of Richland Center. There is also the Potosi Fisheree, the Hodag Country Festival in Rhinelander, Railroad Days in Spooner, Timberfest in Woodruff, Polka Fest in Merrill, Olde Ellison Days in Ellison Bay, the High School Rodeo Finals in Richland Center, Sugar River Days in Broadhead, the Strawberry Festival in Waupaca, Midsummer Fest in Coon Valley, the Heidi Festival in New Glarus, and, in Wausau, a Great Wisconsin River Logjam, "Wood, Wings, Whitewater, and Wausaqua."

July sees Riverfest in La Crosse, the Old Car Show in Iola, Riponfest in Ripon, Pinery Road Days in Adams, the Wisconsin Shakespeare Festival in Platteville, Twin-O-Rama in Cassville (celebrating twins and others of multiple birth), the Bluegill Festival in Birchwood, Honor the Earth Powwow in Hayward, the Blueberry Festival in Iron River, and a War of 1812 Re-enactment in Prairie du Chien.

More? In August, activities range from the Lower Wisconsin River Thresheree Show in Boscobel to the Great River Festival of Traditional Jazz in La Crosse to the Harvest Festival in Muscoda, from the Home of the Hamburger Celebration in Seymour to the Otto Grunski Polski Festyn in Menasha and the Corn 'n Tater Festival in Grand Marsh. Fur and Leather Days take place in Berlin, Aquafest in Wasau, and another Thresheree in Valmy. And, getting the jump on the season, Presque Isle holds its Oktoberfest in August.

The fairs, festivals, and celebrations go well into the fall harvest season, celebrating apples, quilts, crafts, artwork, and more. They continue into the Christmas holiday season, and on into winter. Snowmobile races, cross-country ski races, ice fishing derbies, ice sculpting contests, maple syrup festivals—all continue right up until the end-of-ski-season celebrations in March. Then the celebrations start all over again.

Wisconsin has a lot to celebrate, and it finds no end of ways to do just that.

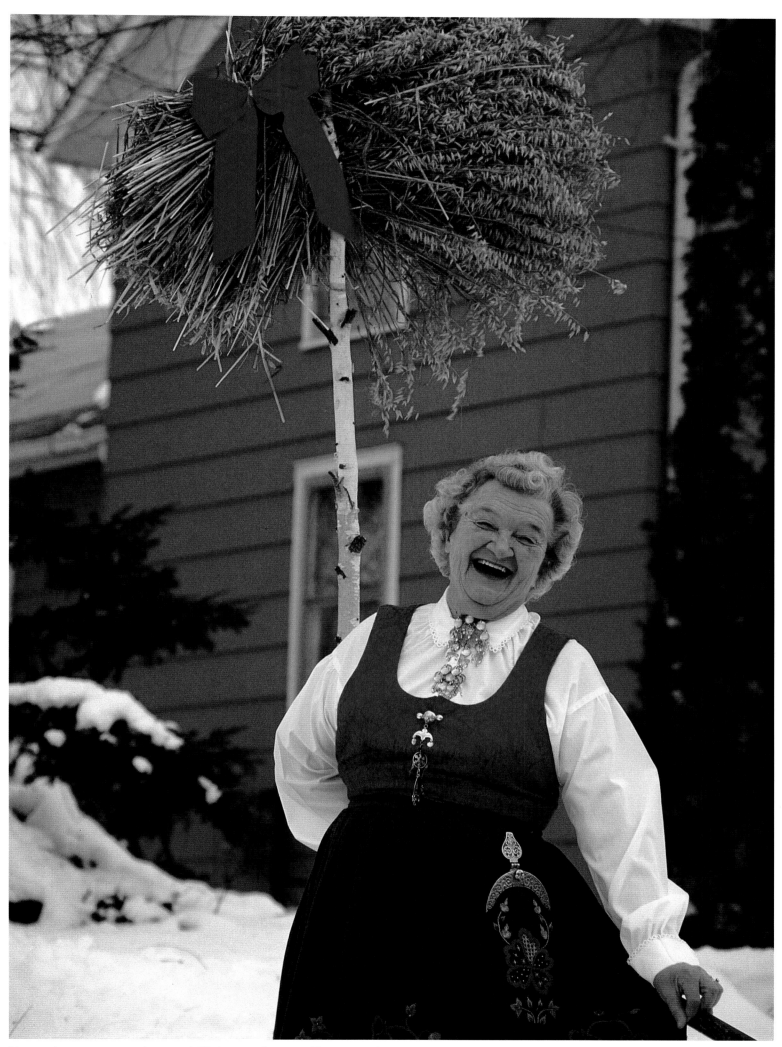

Norwegian customary dress and Christmas sheaves, Blue Mounds

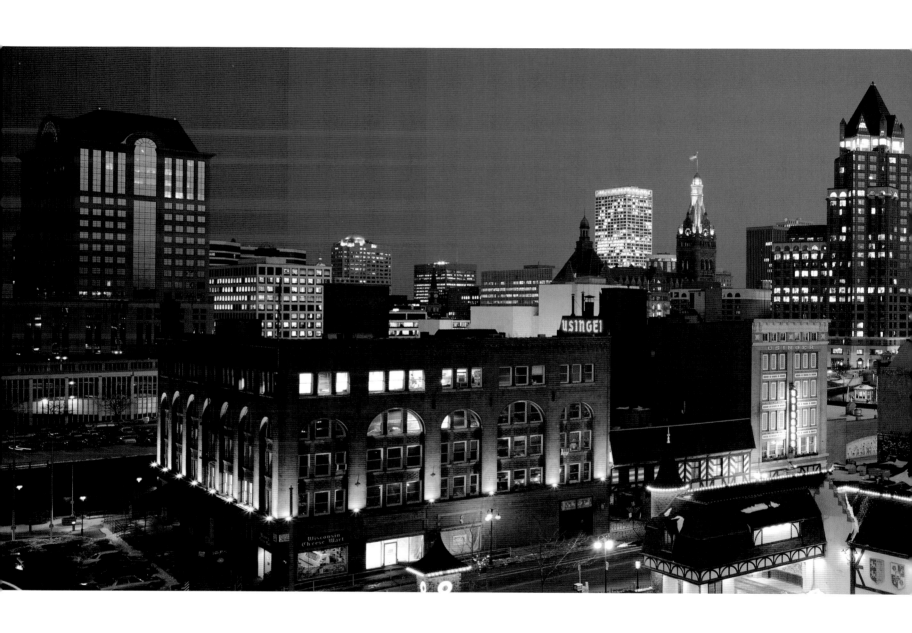

I came here in the 1920s and was overwhelmed with the history of the city, history that is still being made.

OWEN J. GROMME

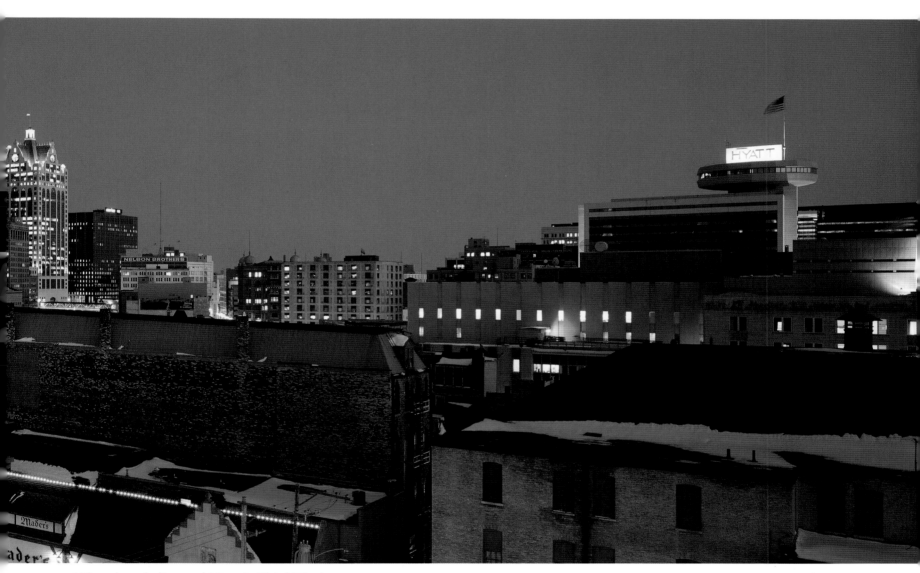

Milwaukee skyline and Historic Third Ward

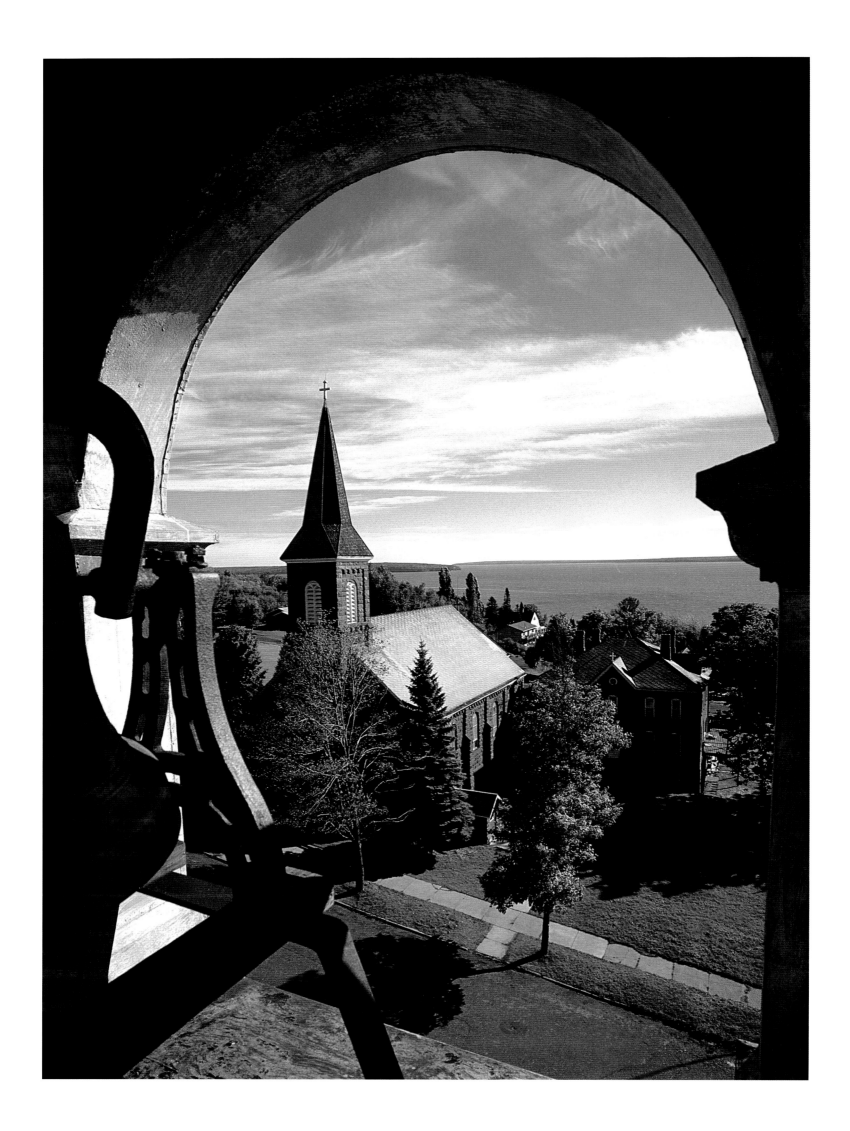

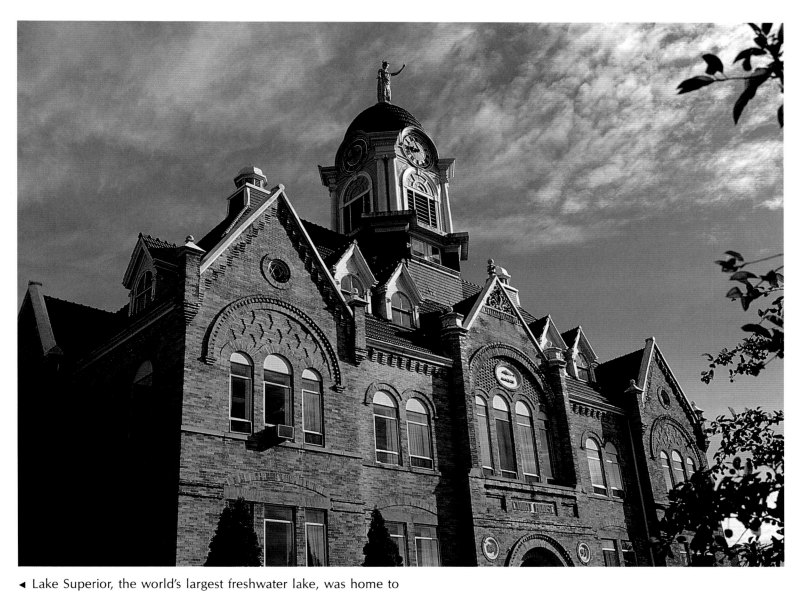

◄ Lake Superior, the world's largest freshwater lake, was home to Native tribes for millennia. The area saw explorers and missionaries arrive in the 1600s, followed by lumberjacks, prospectors, and miners. Bayfield, one of Wisconsin's northernmost cities, is now a destination point for visitors to this scenic and historic area.

▲ With no less than thirty-nine on the National Register, Wisconsin's county courthouses are among the state's essential architectural assets. This singular example of Romanesque revival design, built in 1891, stands in Oconto on the western shore of Green Bay.

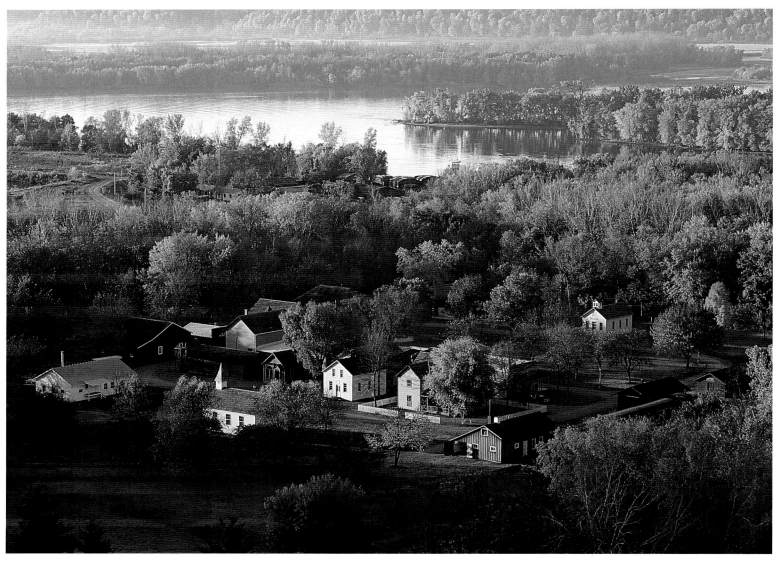

▲ Stonefield Village was recreated by the State Historical Society to depict life in the 1890s. The site, named for the first governor, is part of Nelson Dewey State Park, in the state's southwesternmost corner. ▶ The Italianate Edwin Galloway House in Fond du Lac, built in 1846, is one of more than fourteen hundred sites in Wisconsin now listed in the National Register of Historic Places.

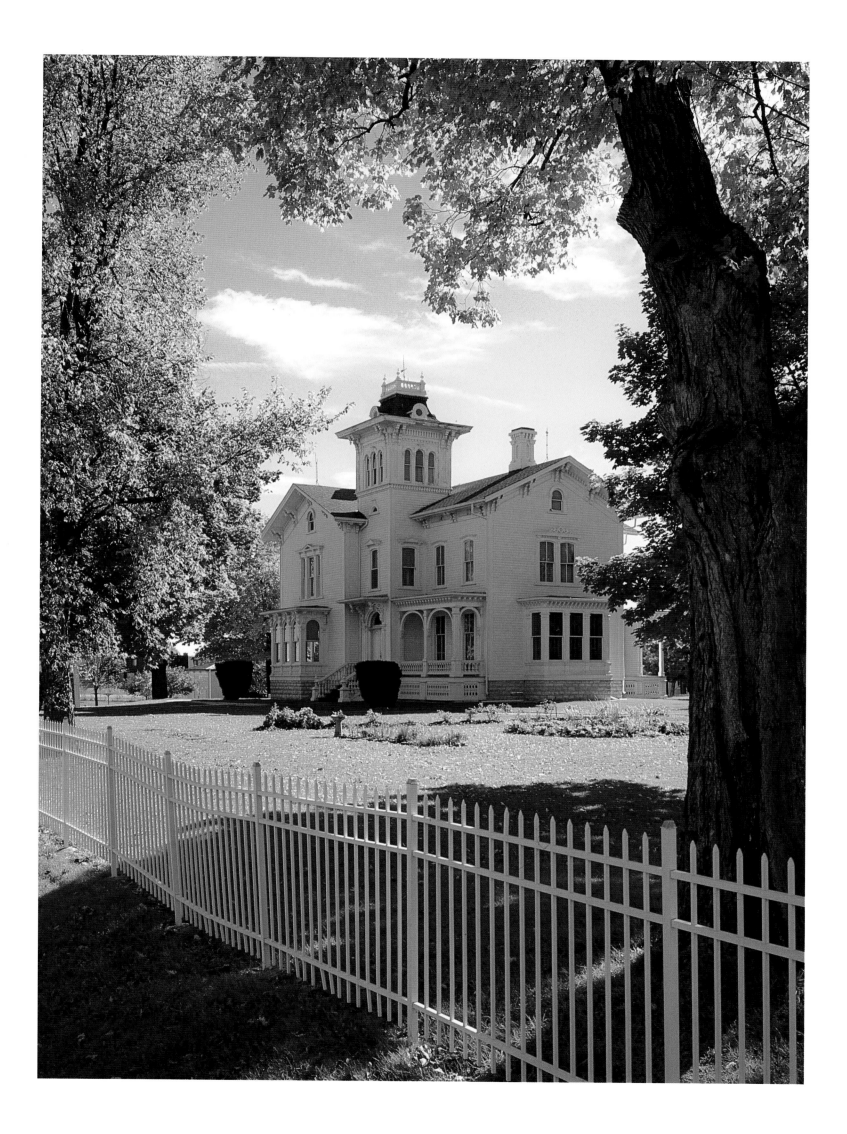

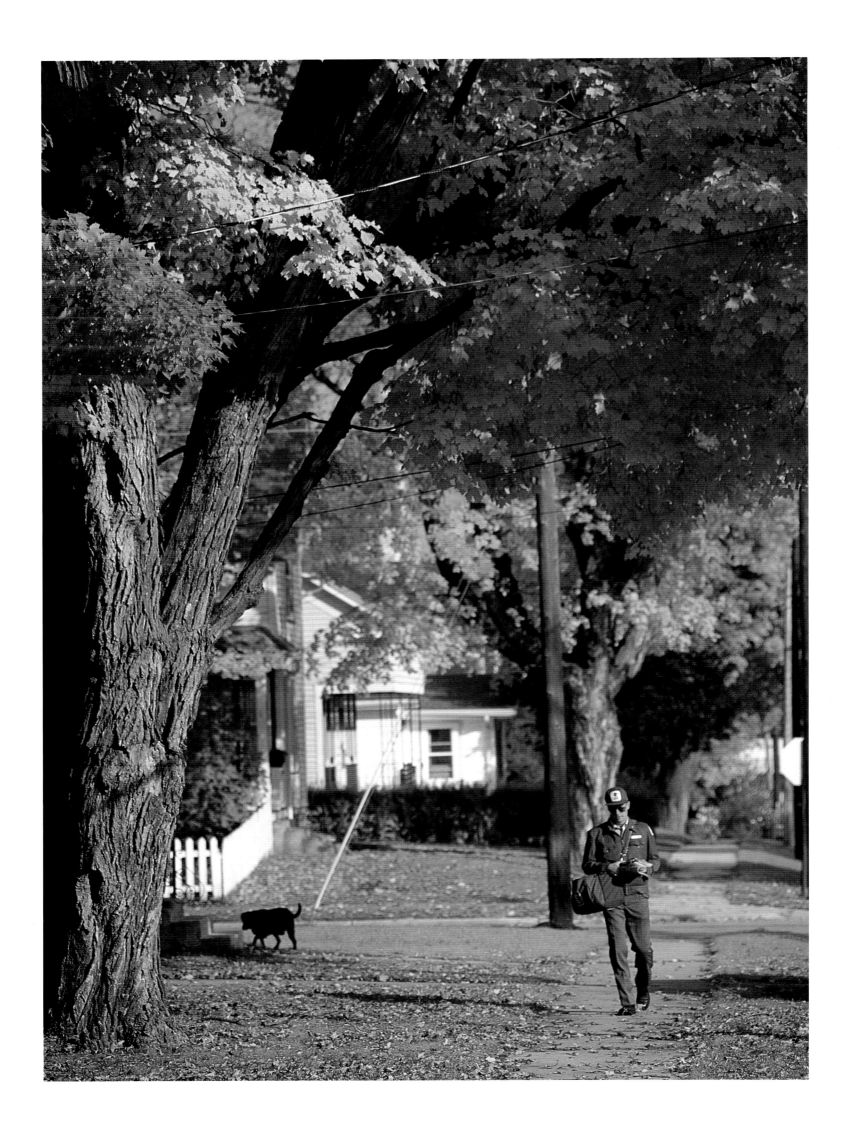

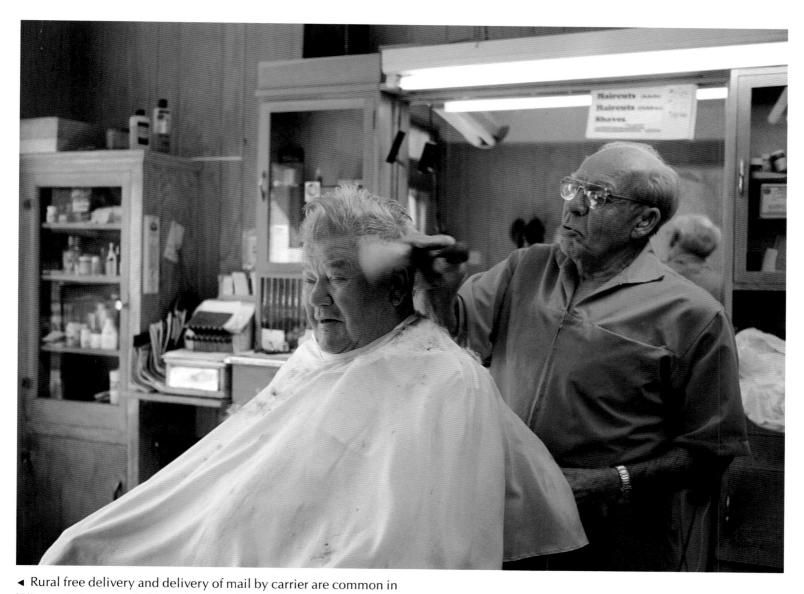

◄ Rural free delivery and delivery of mail by carrier are common in Wisconsin towns and cities where service predates curbside boxes.
▲ Wisconsin's greatest natural resource is undoubtedly its people. From Wisconsin minds have come the legends of Paul Bunyan, the nation's first workmen's compensation law, and the "Wisconsin Idea," where government and education exist for all its citizens. Birthplace of the Republican Party, as well as the Gideons and the Freethinkers Society, it is also the home of the Burlington Liar's Club.

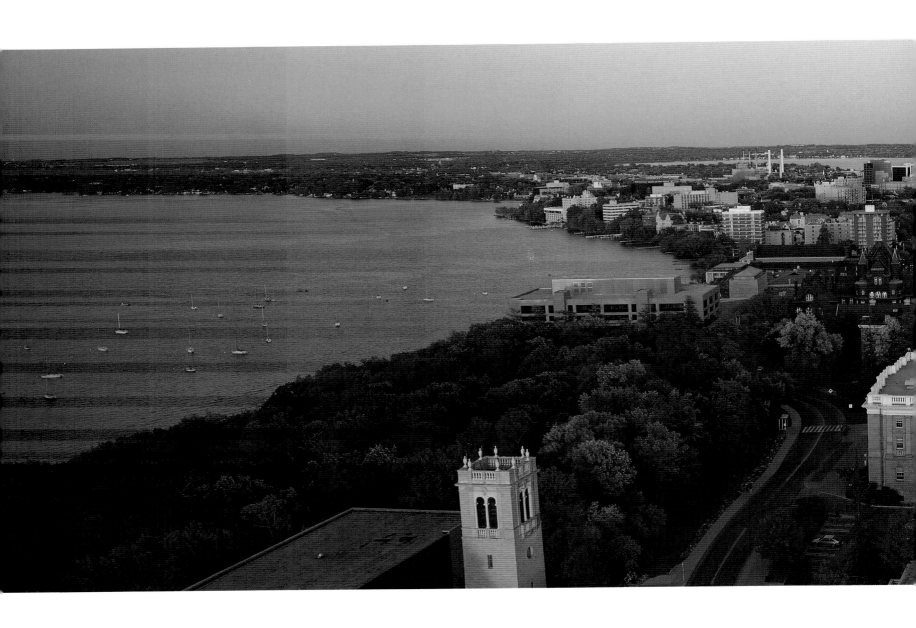

I came to the university in the 1940s and the boundaries of the university were the boundaries of the state, everything radiated out from this campus.

ROBERT E. GARD

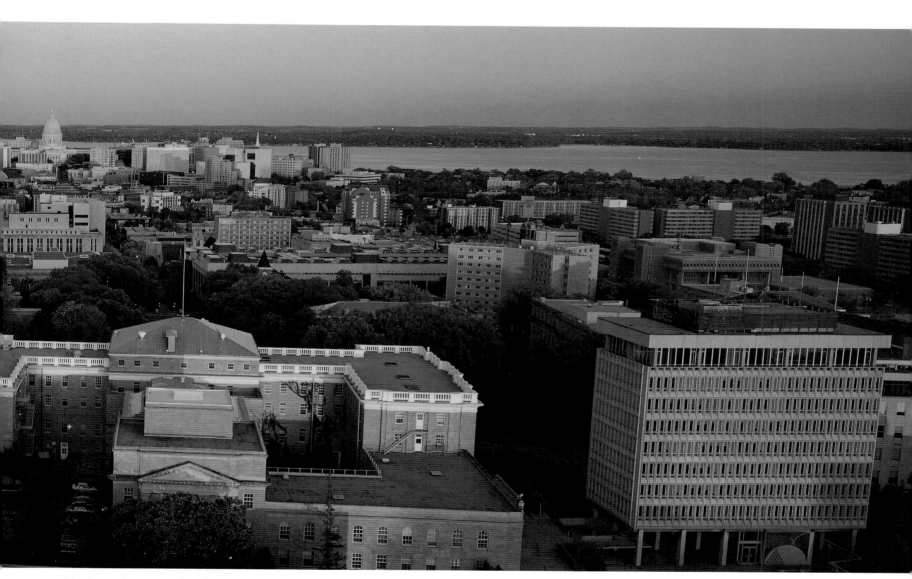

Madison skyline with Lakes Mendota and Monona

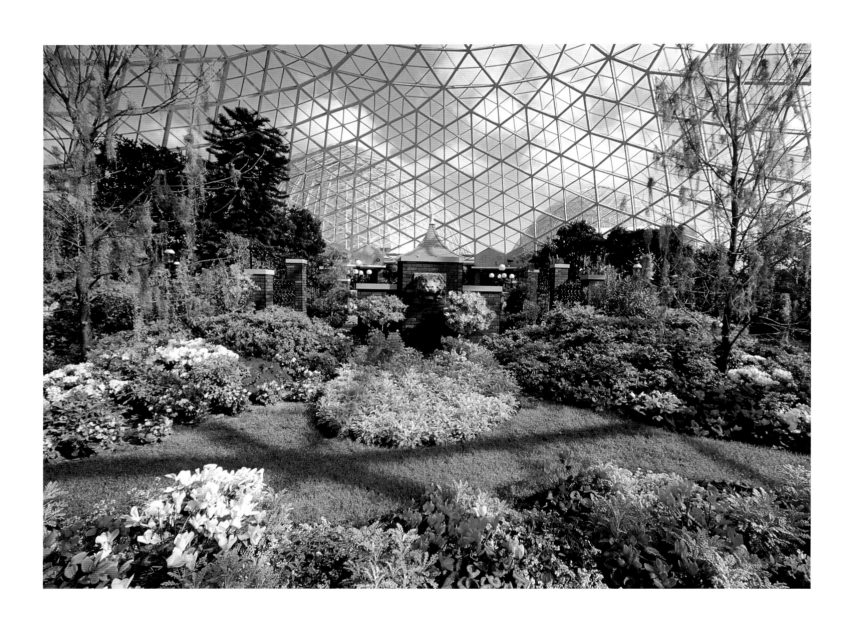

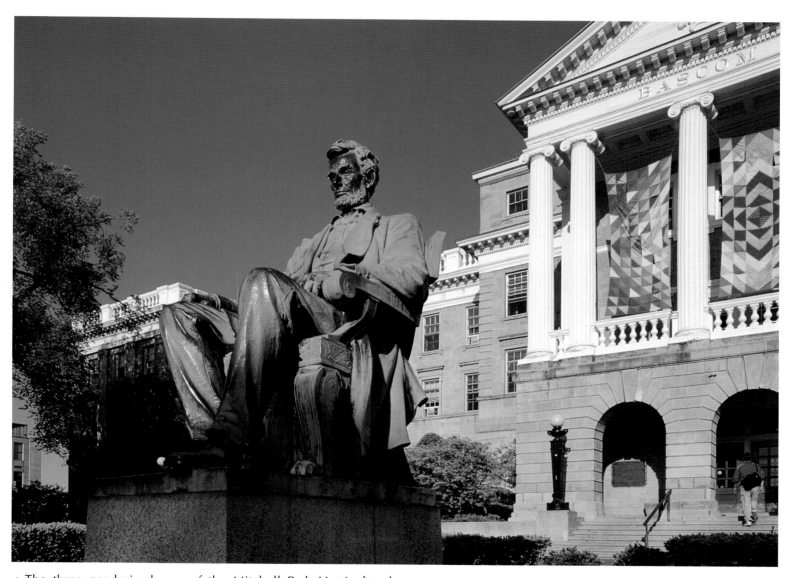

◄ The three geodesic domes of the Mitchell Park Horticultural Conservatory in Milwaukee are each the height of a seven-story building and half the length of a football field. The Tropical and Desert Domes maintain their displays throughout the year, while the Show Dome frequently changes its spectacular floral exhibit.
▲ Bascom Hall and Lincoln Terrace are situated atop Bascom Hill in Madison, home to the University of Wisconsin, established in 1848. It is now one of the ten largest and most distinguished systems in the country, with twenty-six campuses across the state.

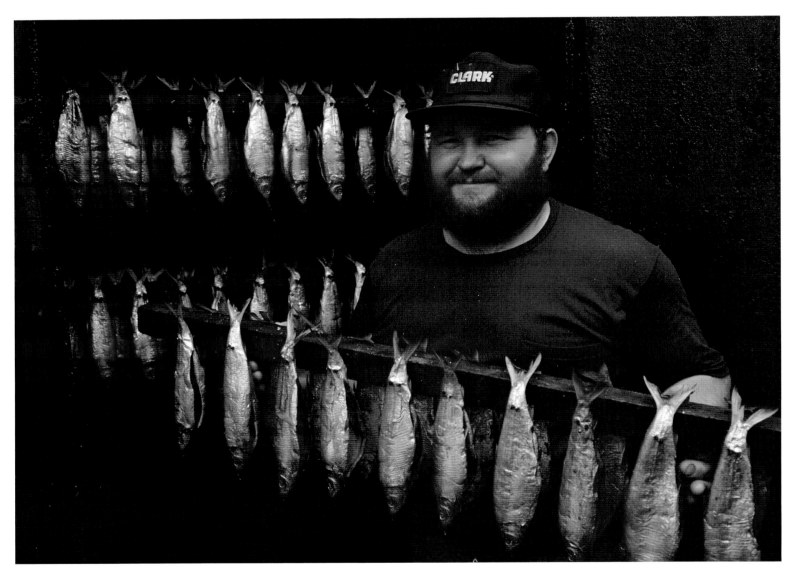

▲ Situated on the eastern coast of the Door Peninsula, Algoma has often laid claim to record lake salmon catches just off its shores. A smaller delicacy, the chub, is a favorite with many when smoked.

► Given the great many rivers flowing through the state and its gateway ports on two Great Lakes, it is only natural that boat building in Wisconsin has had a long and prosperous history. With the demise of some of the larger yards between Milwaukee and Chicago, enterprising individuals have found success more recently working on hand-crafted wooden boats.

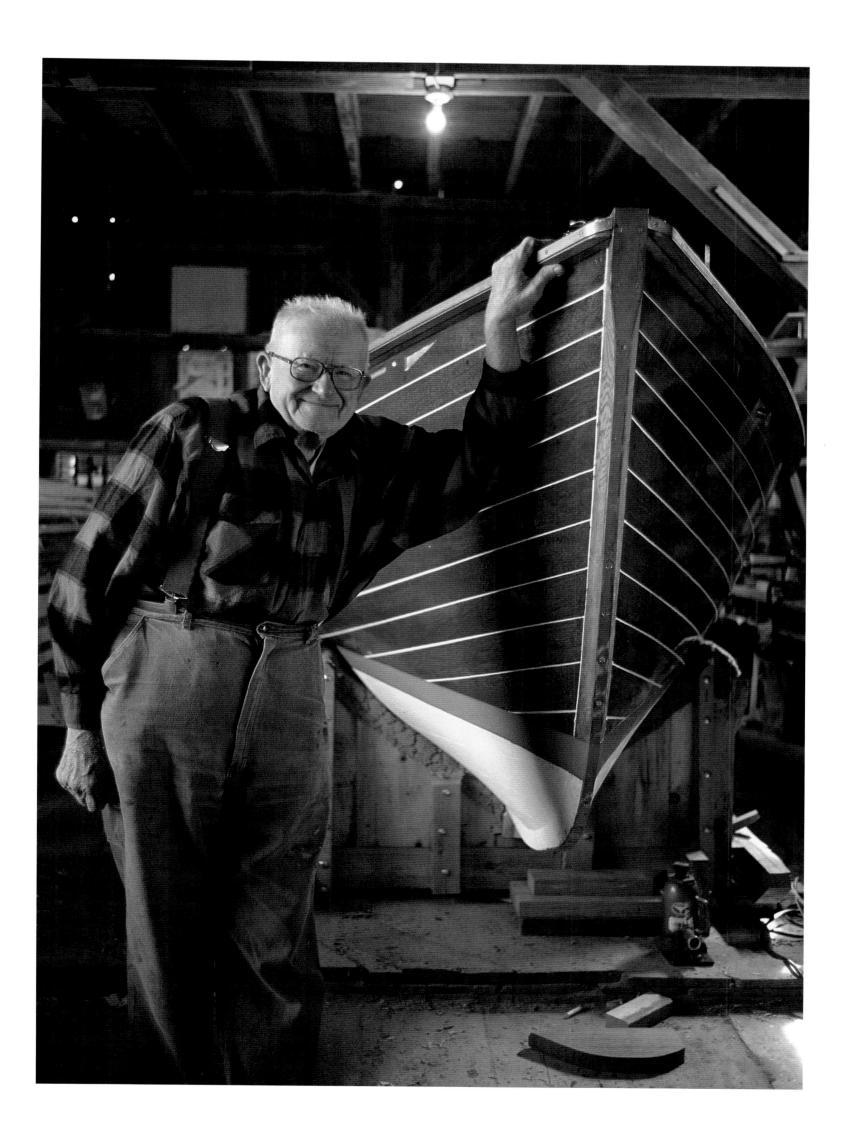

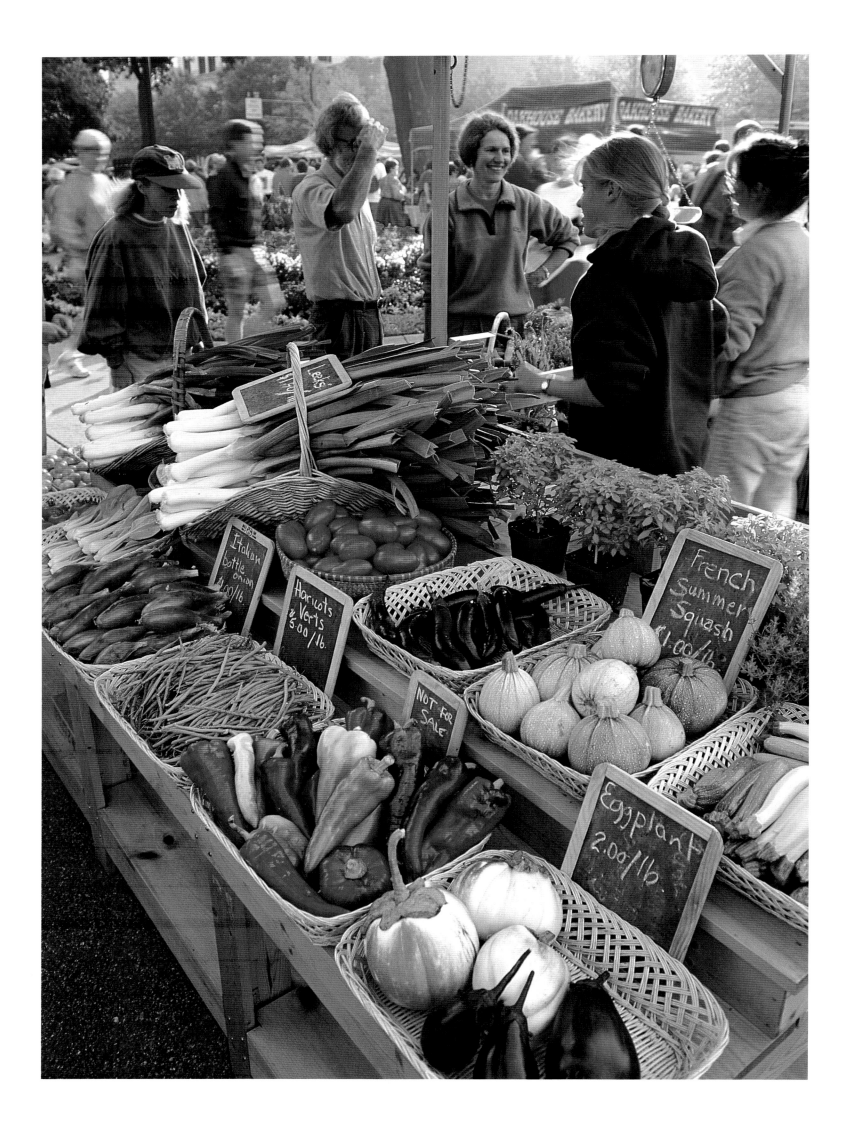

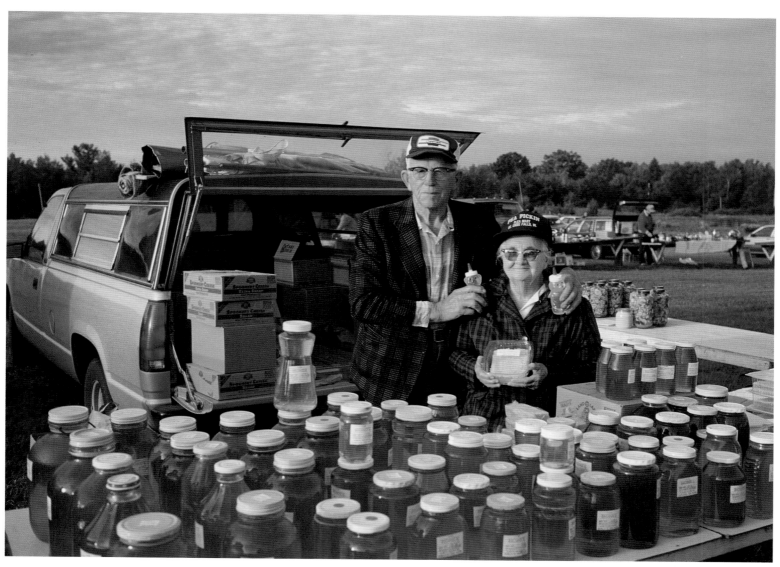

◄ Established in the mid-1970s, the Dane County Farmers Market on the Square was one of the first statewide farmers markets and is now a veritable social institution on Saturday mornings. Extending from early May into November, these markets have become outlets for fresh commercial and organic produce from area growers.
▲ The flea market is ubiquitous in Wisconsin, sometimes occurring weekly, sometimes monthly. It is an opportunity for meeting friends, buying staples, and finding occasional lost treasure.

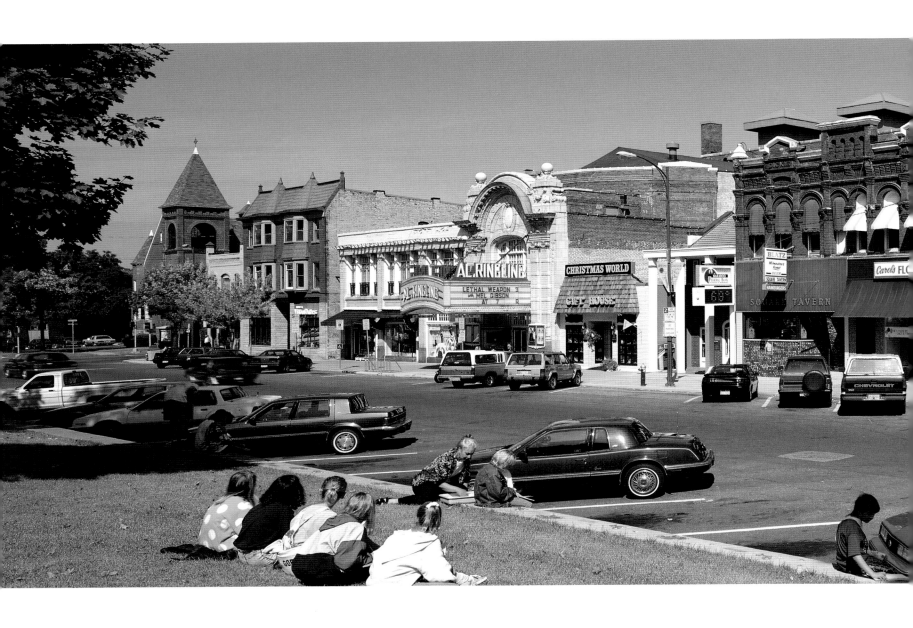

The city square is the heart of America's small towns. It is where we linger, remember and come together.

AUGUST DERLETH

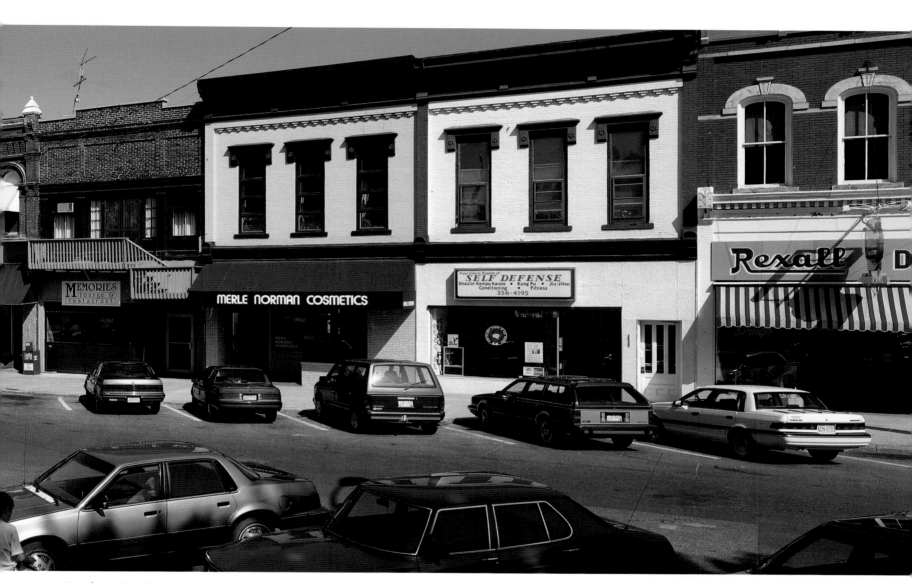

Baraboo City Square

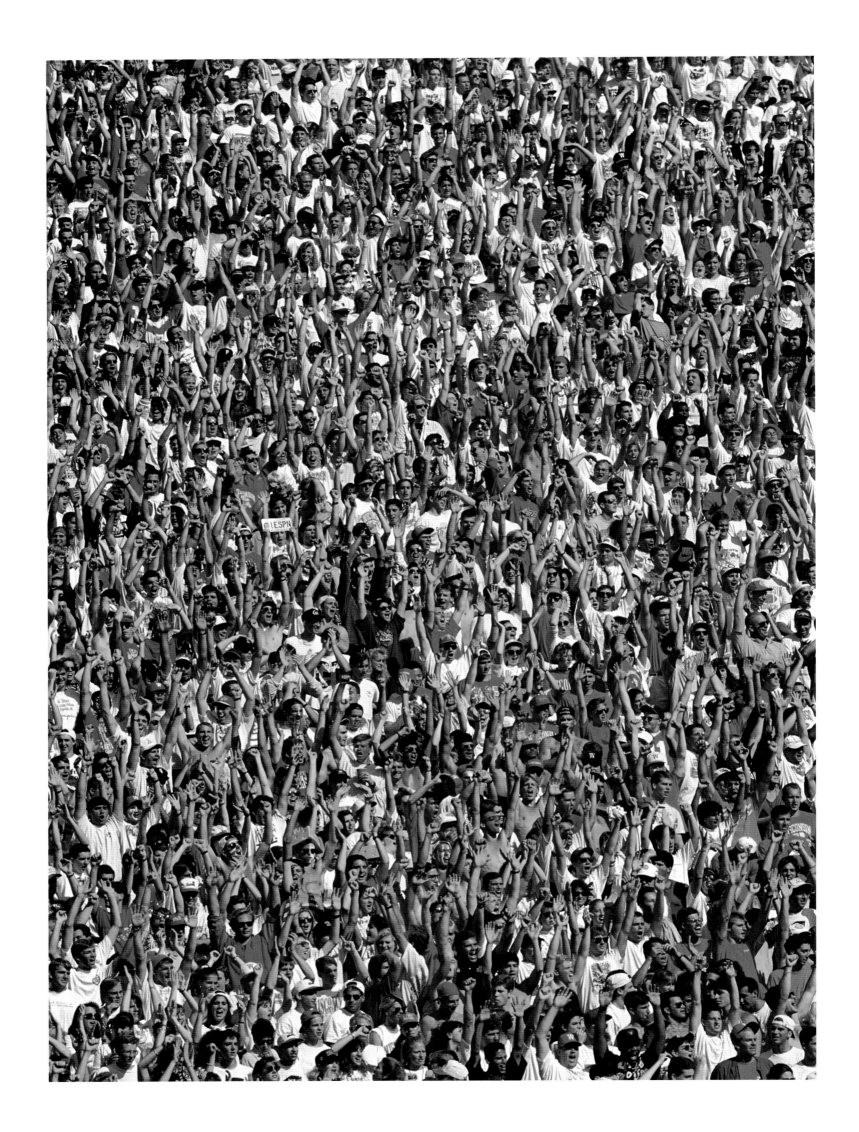

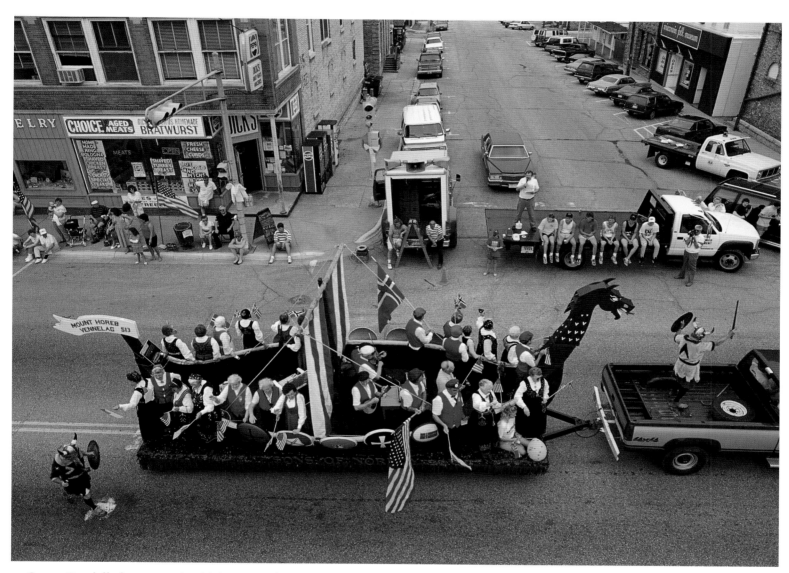

◄ Camp Randall, home to the University of Wisconsin football Badgers, is the eleventh-largest college-owned stadium, with a seating capacity of 77,745. During the Civil War, Camp Randall acted as a government military training center for seventy thousand troops.
▲ Wisconsin suffers no shortage of good parades, particularly the ethnically inspired, from the Norwegian Summer Parade down the main street of Mount Horeb to the Great Circus Parade through the streets of Milwaukee, where over a million spectators watch.

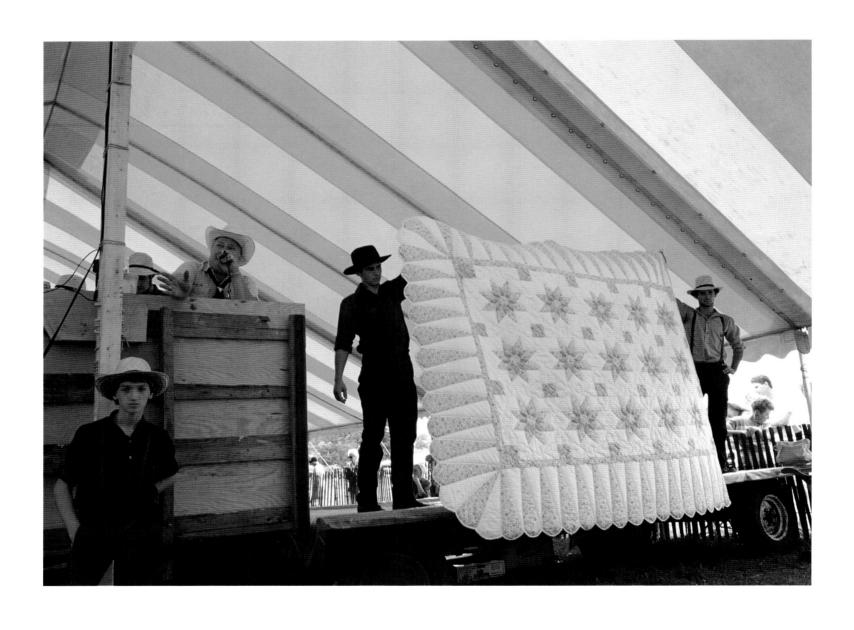

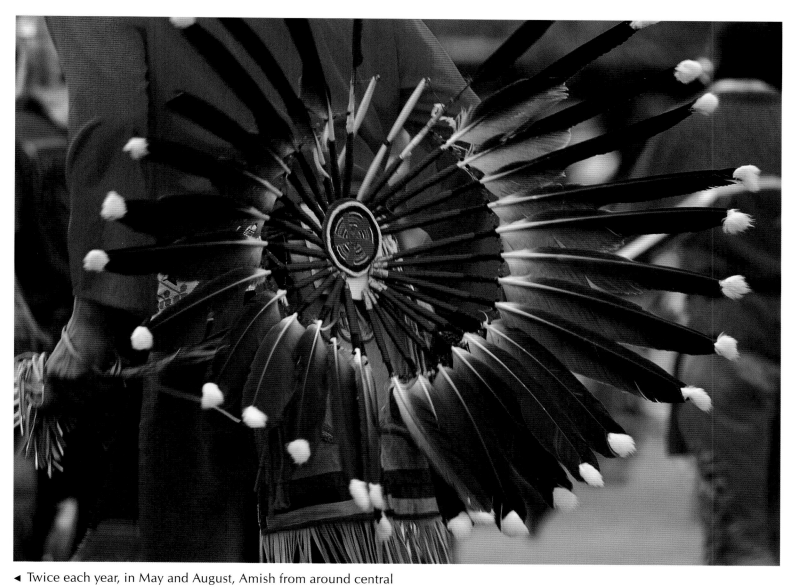

◄ Twice each year, in May and August, Amish from around central Wisconsin gather outside of Amherst Junction in Portage County for an old-fashioned quilt and consignment auction. Kind people and good neighbors, the Amish have sensitized state government on issues concerning schooling and separation of church and state.

▲ The "Honor the Earth" Pow Wow is held on the Lac Court Oreilles Reservation, home to fifteen hundred Chippewa. Covering nearly seventy thousand acres, this area of abundant game, fish, and wild rice was favored by the Sioux and Ottawa before the Ojibwe arrived in 1745. Wisconsin is home to ten Native tribes.

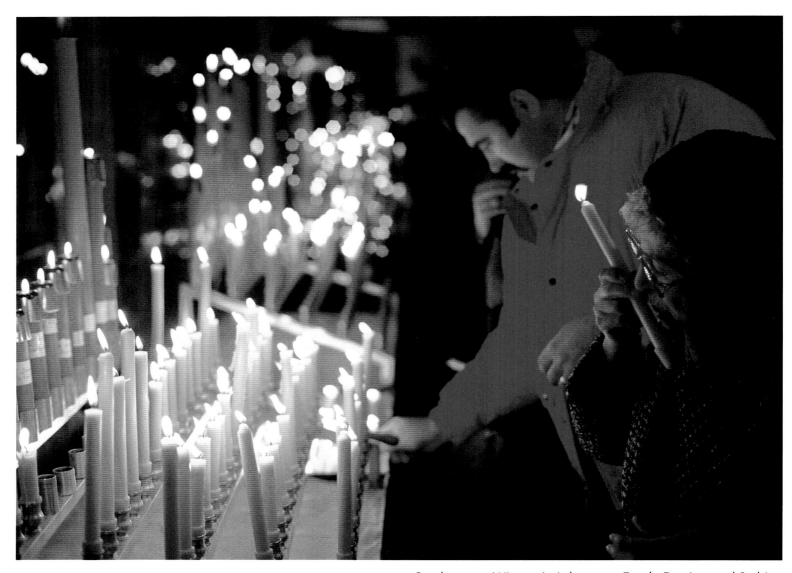

▲ Southeastern Wisconsin is home to Greek, Russian, and Serbian Orthodox communities, as well as other Eastern European religious minorities. At St. Sava in Milwaukee, Christmas Eve is celebrated on January 6 with candlelighting and traditional Serbian Mass.
▶ Santa Lucia Day, December 13, is a Swedish holiday marking the beginning of Christmas celebrations in many Swedish homes across the state. Lucia is a symbol of light and hope; the day commemorates her martyrdom in the fourth-century Roman Empire.

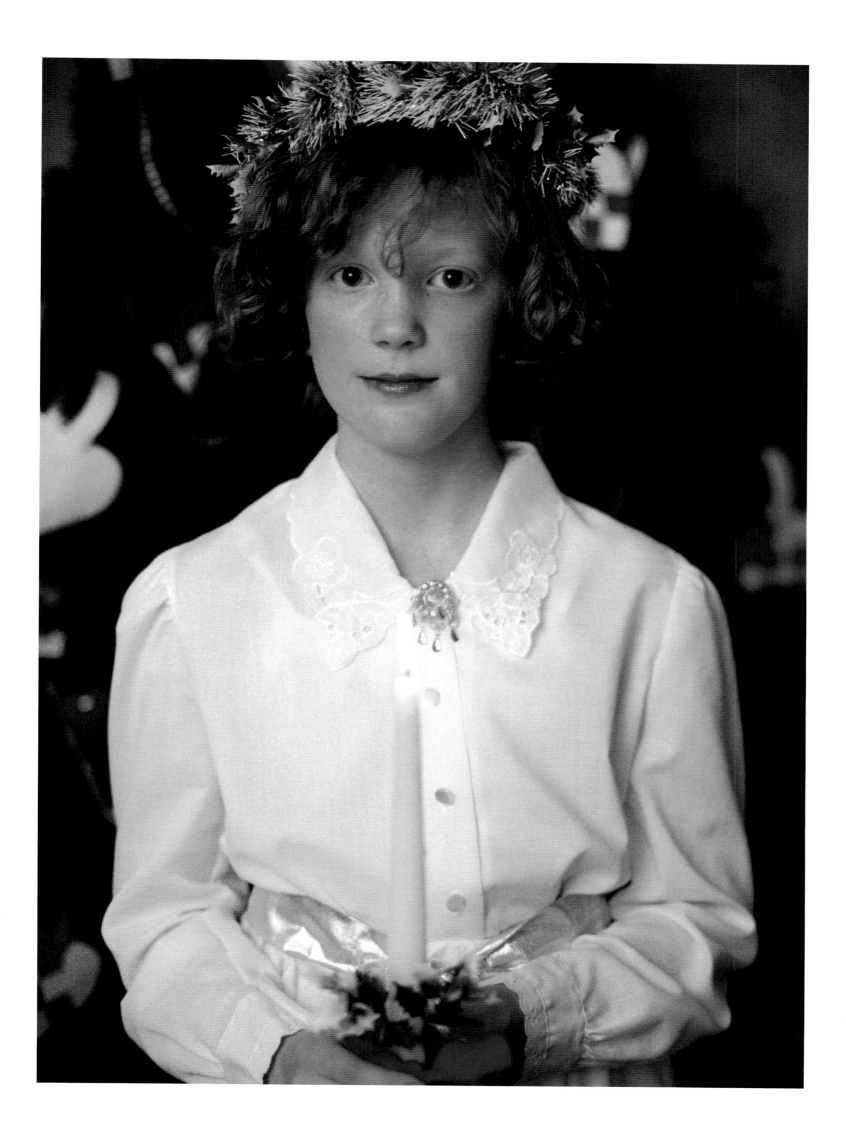

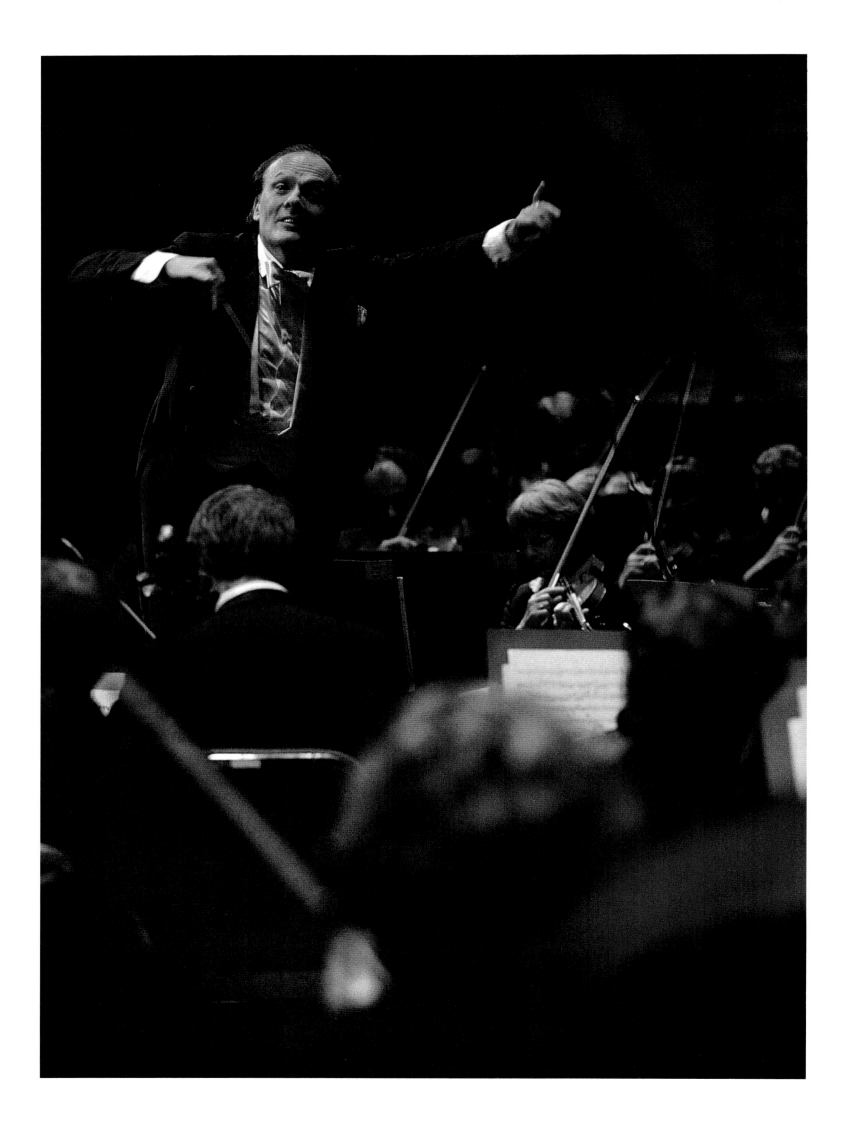

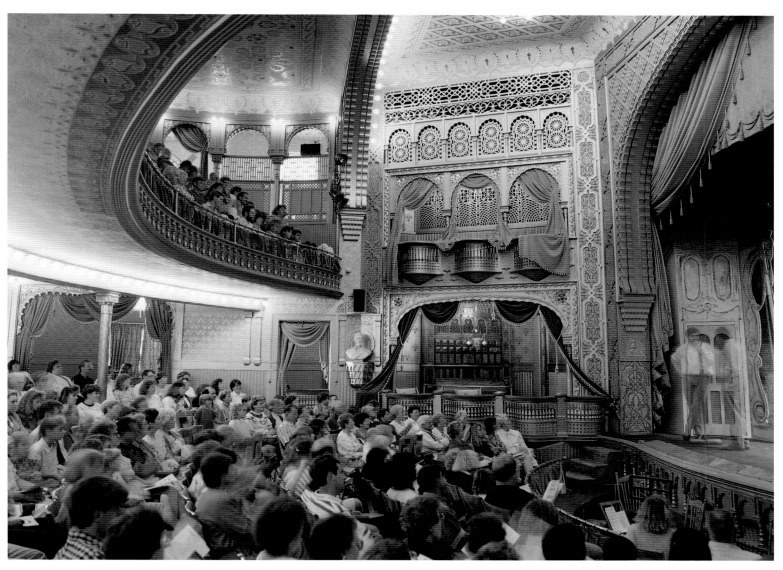

◄ Wisconsin's largest city, Milwaukee is home to the renowned Milwaukee Symphony Orchestra, as well as one of the country's best natural history museums—the Milwaukee Public Museum—and the Milwaukee Art Museum designed by architect Eero Saarinen.
▲ Built in the 1890s and exuding a Moorish influence, the Mabel Tainter Memorial Theater in Menomonee features hand-carved and hand-stenciled decoration, and the original Steere and Turner pipe organ. Its seating is in the style of the New York Opera House.

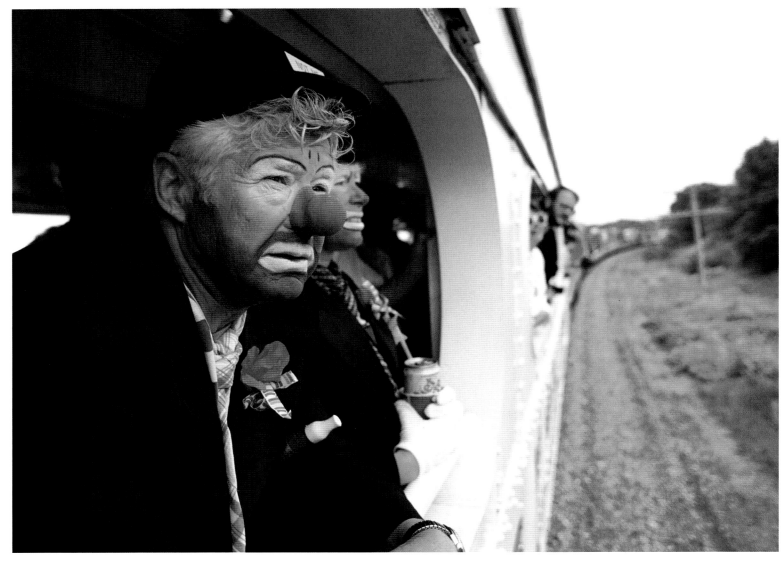

▲ To commemorate Wisconsin's role as the birthplace of more than one hundred circuses—including P. T. Barnum and Ringling Brothers—the Circus World Museum was established by the State Historical Society of Wisconsin in the old Ringling barns in Baraboo in 1959. In July, the Circus Train travels through southern Wisconsin, culminating in the Great Circus Parade through Milwaukee's streets.
▶ In the northwoods town of Phillips, Fred Smith created more than two hundred huge figures of animals and people, using cement, broken beer bottles, and glass knobs. Scenes are taken from history and local folklore. Fred was sixty-three when he started.

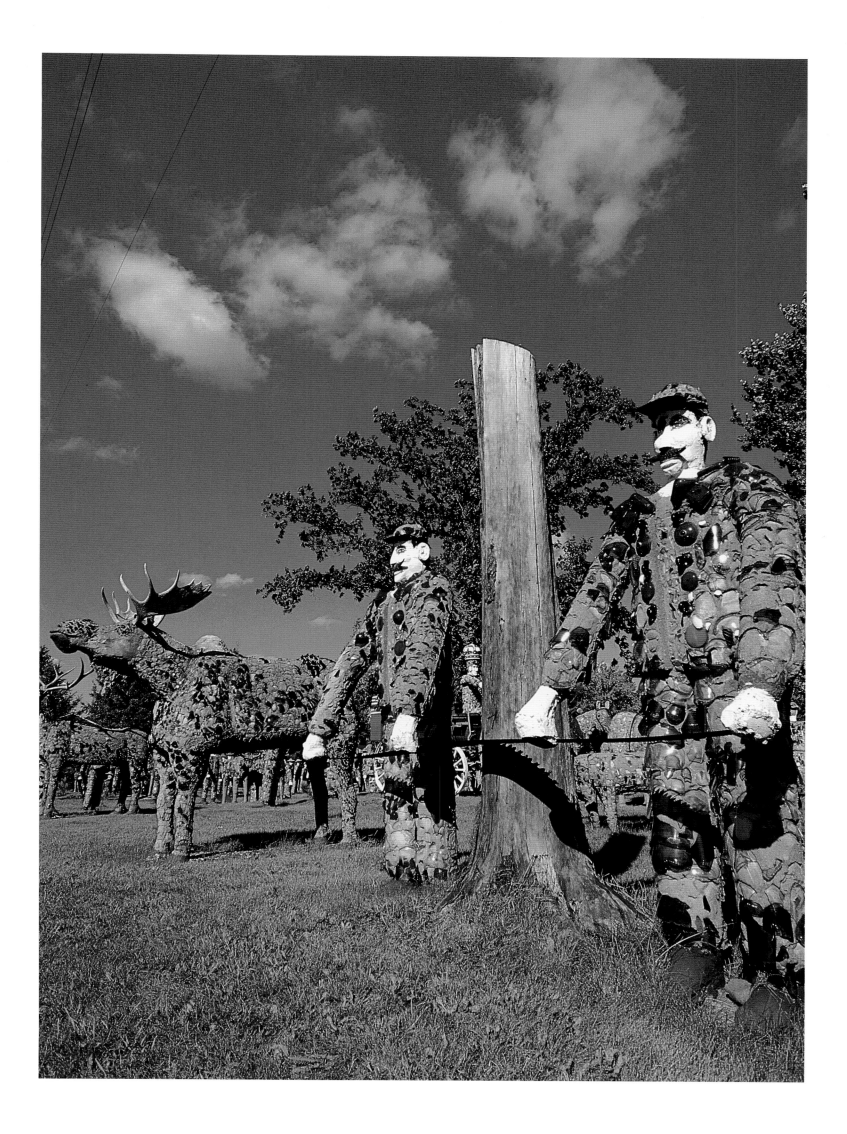

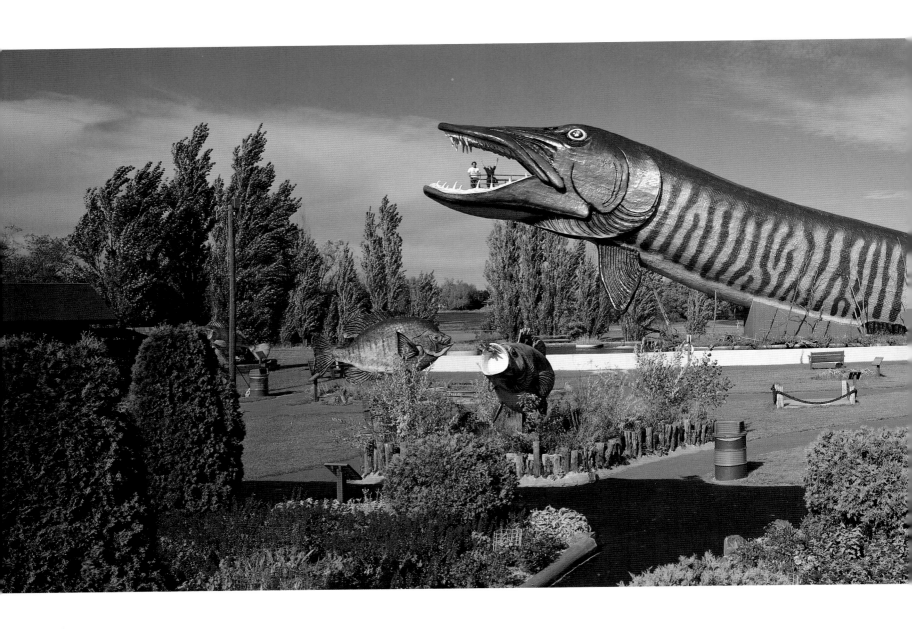

All fishing is a spiritual thing.
SIGURD OLSON

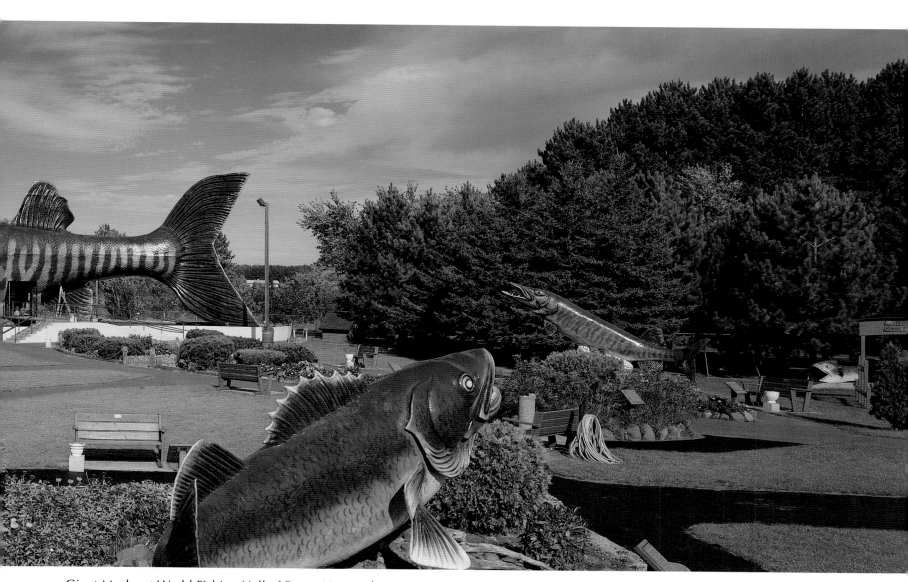

Giant Musky at World Fishing Hall of Fame, Hayward

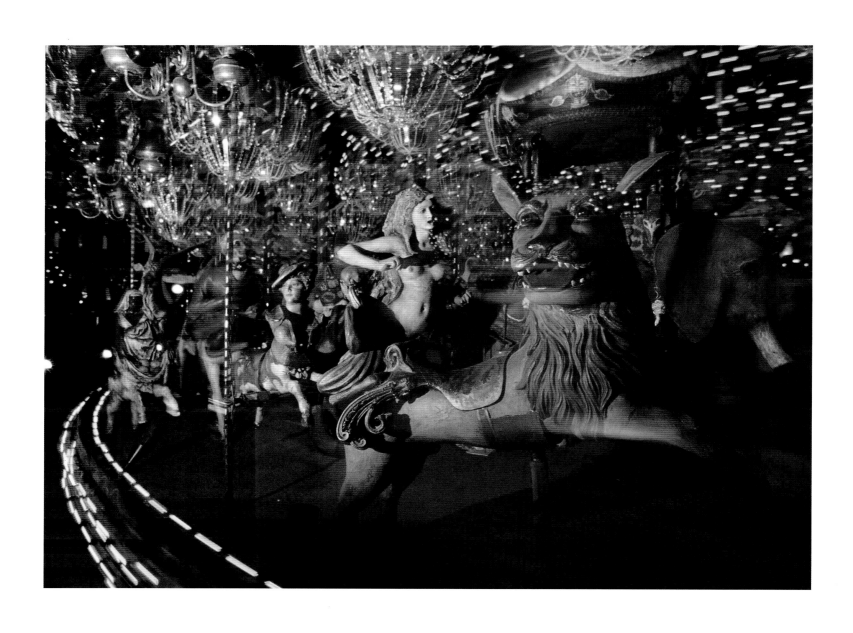

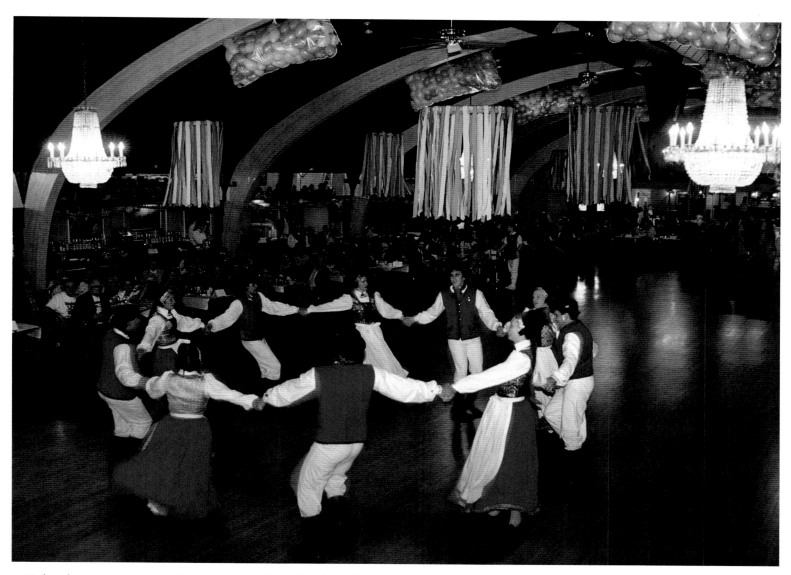

◄ Eighty feet across, with 269 animals—both real and mythical—the largest carousel in the world occupies one of the sixteen complexes at the House on the Rock in Iowa County's Wyoming Valley.
▲ Octoberfest, a German folk festival that began in Bavaria in 1810 to honor the marriage of Prince Ludwig I and Princess Therese, is still an honored tradition in Wisconsin's German communities.
► ► In winter, the action of wind, cold, and water creates massive ice formations in the rocks and caves of the Apostle Islands National Lakeshore, off Bayfield Peninsula. This national park encompasses twenty-one islands and a twelve-mile stretch of wild mainland.

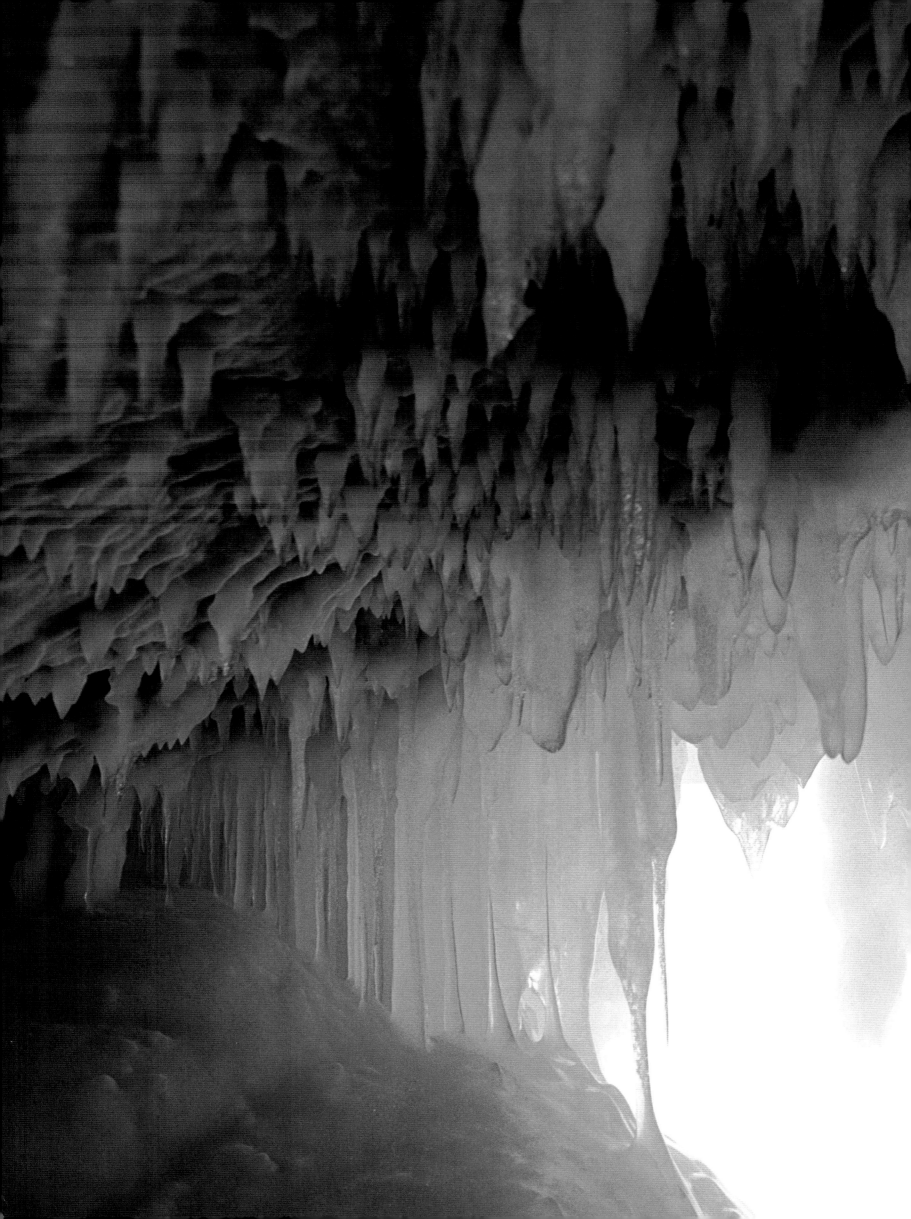

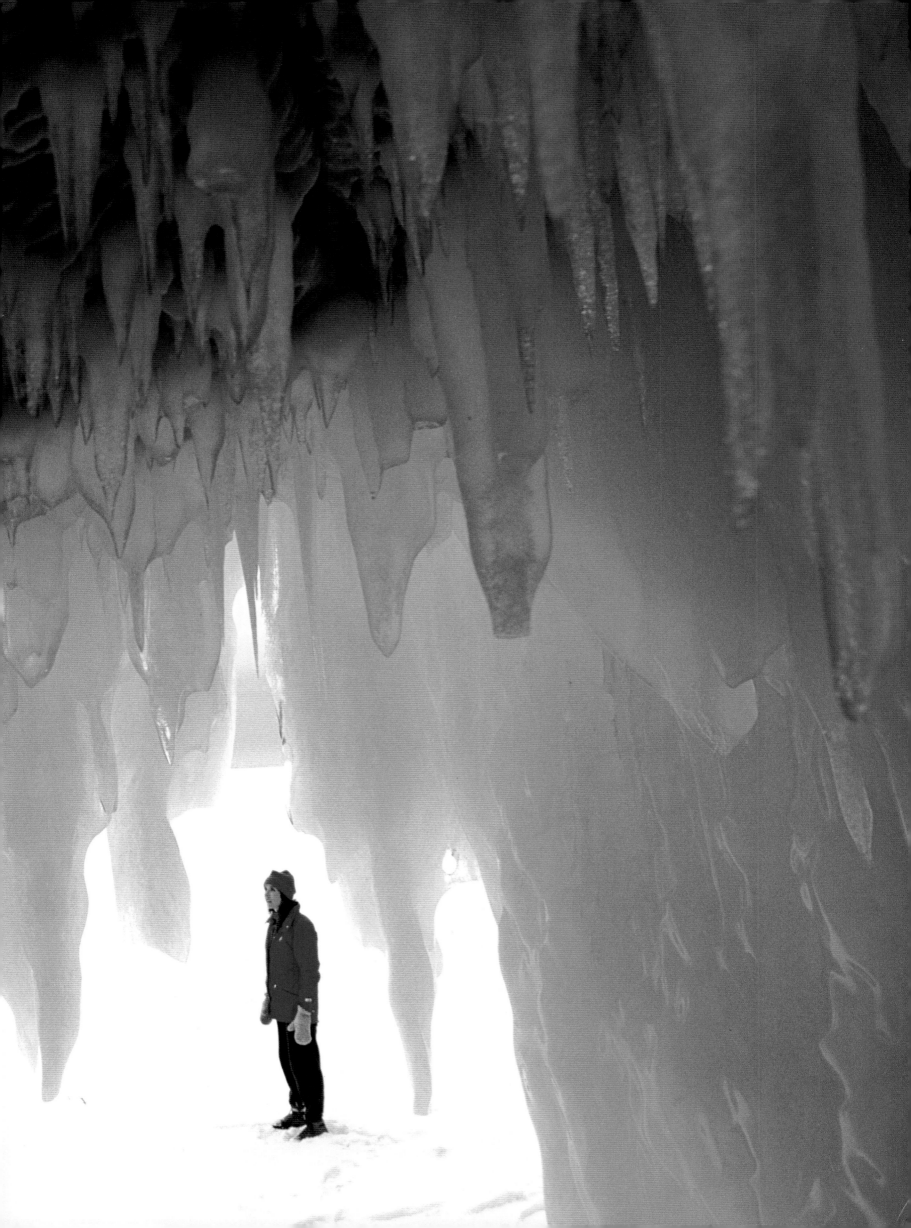

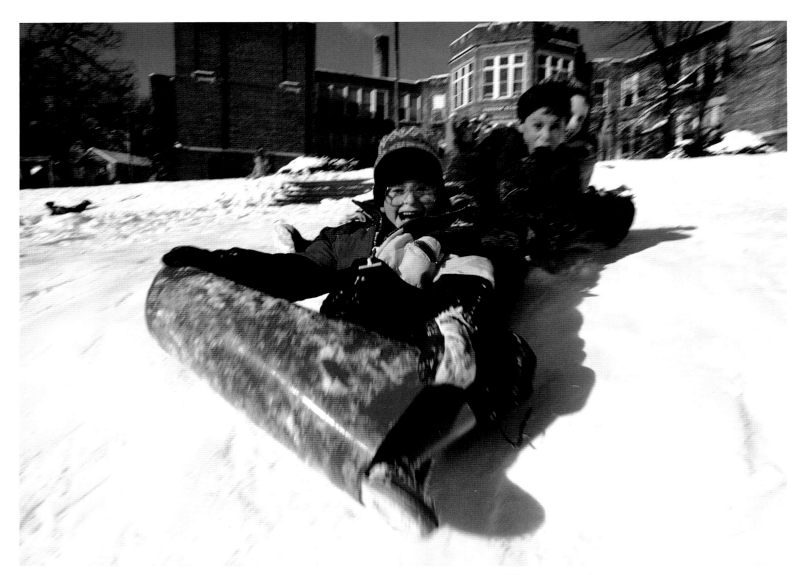

▲ Frequent snowfalls averaging four inches or more are common in the southern part of the state, though total snowfall can vary greatly from one year to the next. Sledders and skiers in the northern part of the state are guaranteed great conditions for most of the winter.
▶ The American Birkebeiner, known as the "Birkie," is a fifty-five-kilometer cross-country ski race near Cable and Hayward. Modeled after the Norwegian ski race, it is North America's largest cross-country ski event, bringing in thousands of amateur and world-class professionals for what has become an annual Nordic festival.

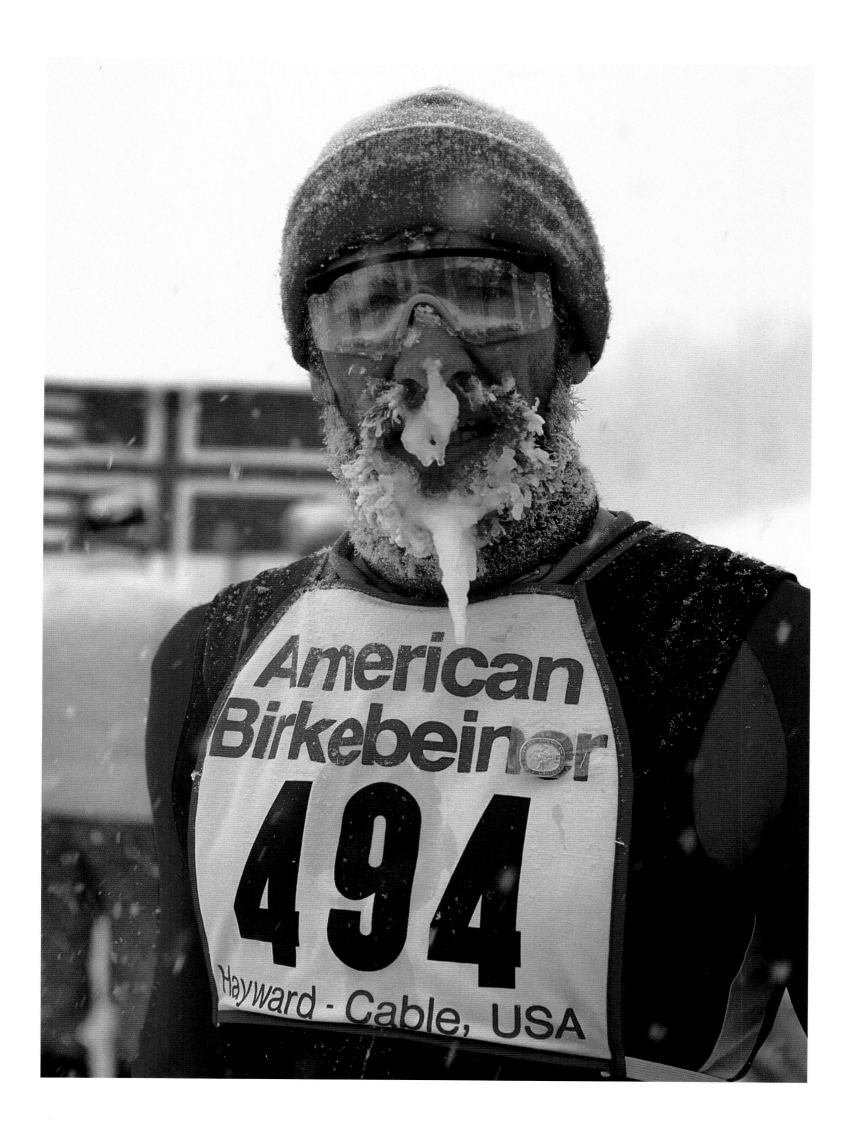

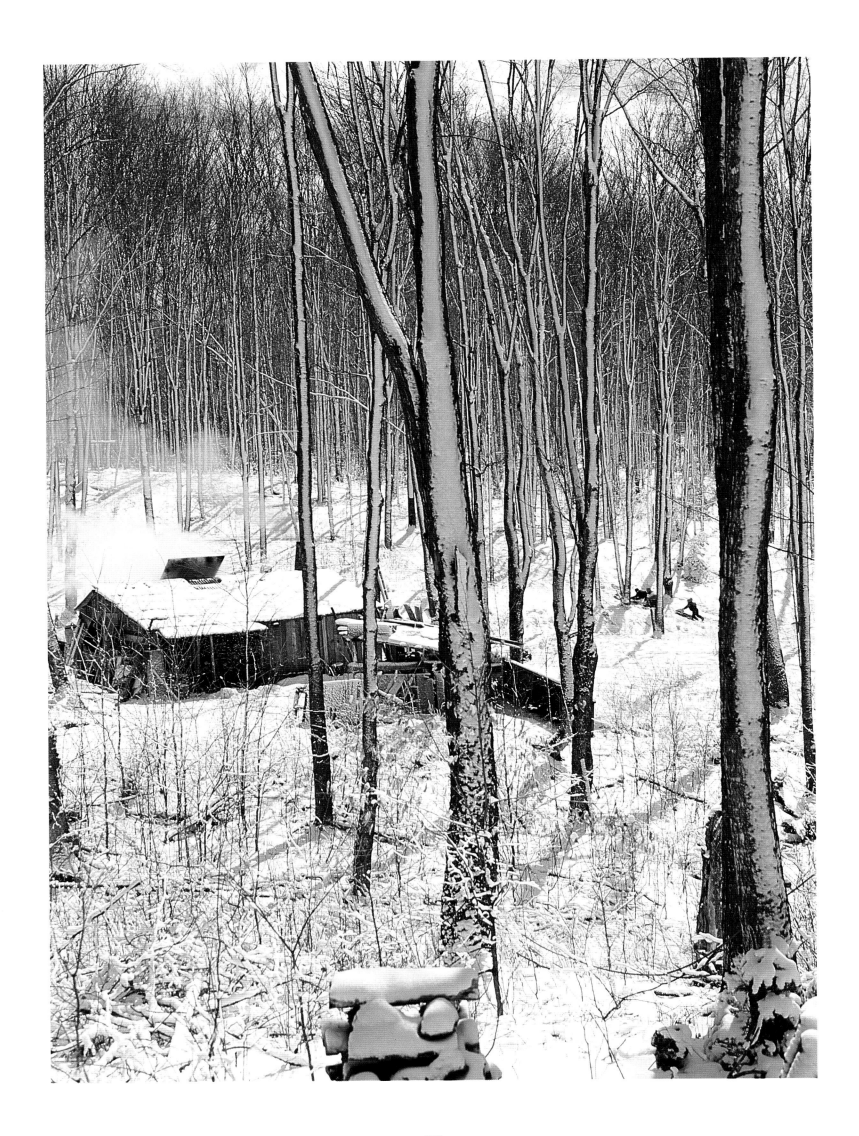

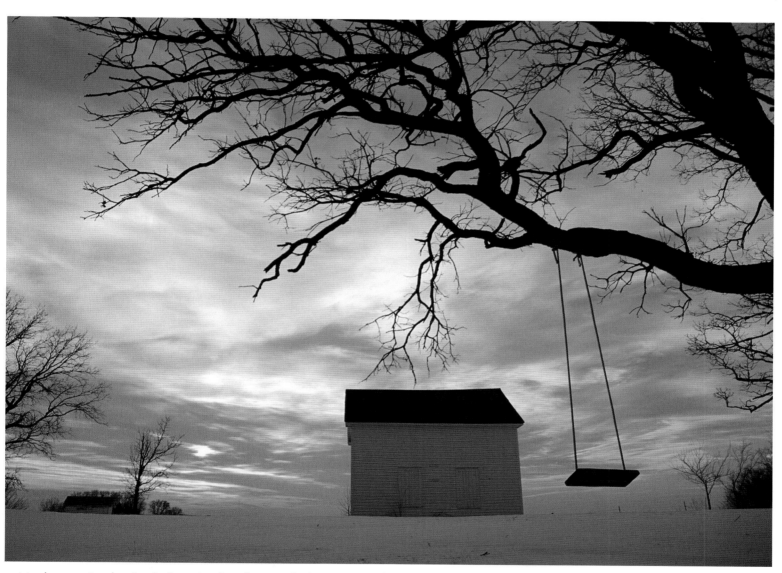

◄ Maple sugaring begins before the first thaw with the tapping of mature maple trees. It is the first-run sap from early in the season, when nights are still cold, that produces the most delicate syrup.
▲ Built of oak logs in 1852, the eighteen-by-eighteen-foot Hauge Log Church near Daleyville was one of the earliest Norwegian Lutheran churches in Wisconsin. Though the exterior has been clapboarded over, the church's interior is original: lime plaster over log walls, combined pulpit and altar, and homemade pews.

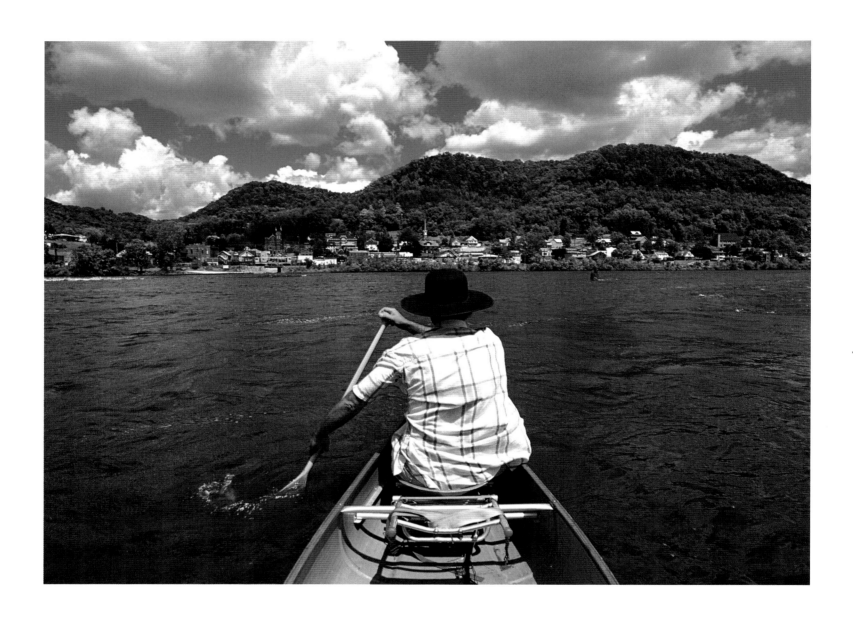

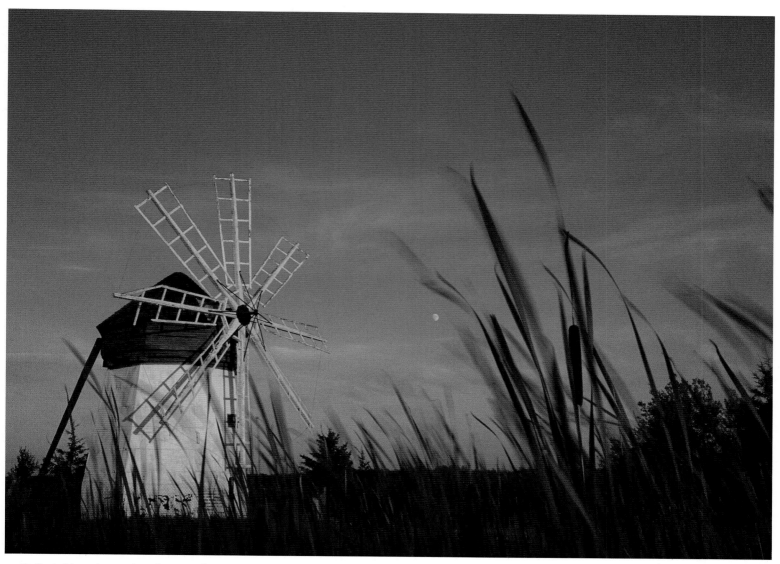

◄ Called "the river of a thousand voices," the Mississippi River passes close to small towns such as Fountain City and parallels Highway 35, the Great River Road, from St. Paul to Cassville.
▲ The Davidson Windmill in Douglas County was built by Finnish settlers in 1900 and was based on a traditional rural Finnish design. The log turret revolves with the bladed wheel so that it can be turned into the wind. It is the last windmill still standing in Wisconsin.

We would sit out in those shacks and meditate like Buddhas on the ice.

GEORGE VUKELICH

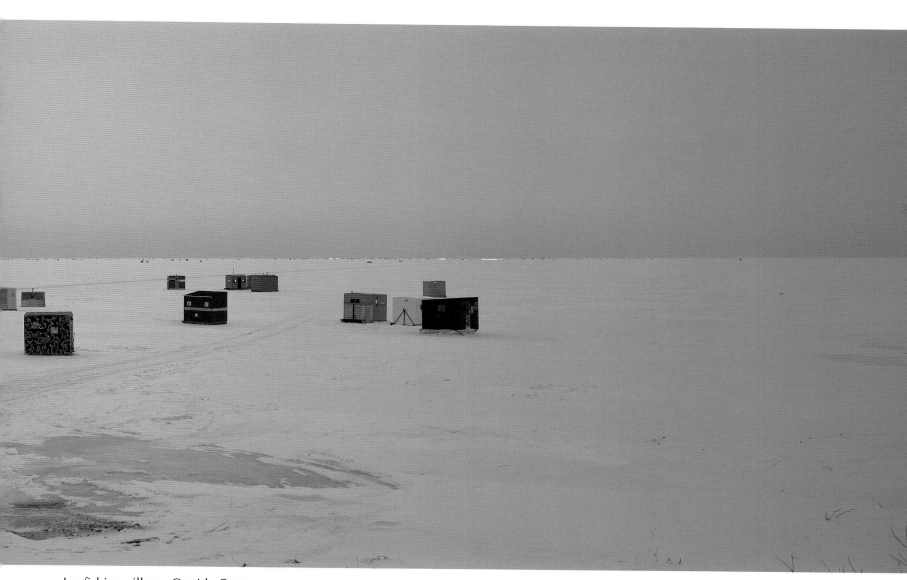

Ice fishing village, Oneida County

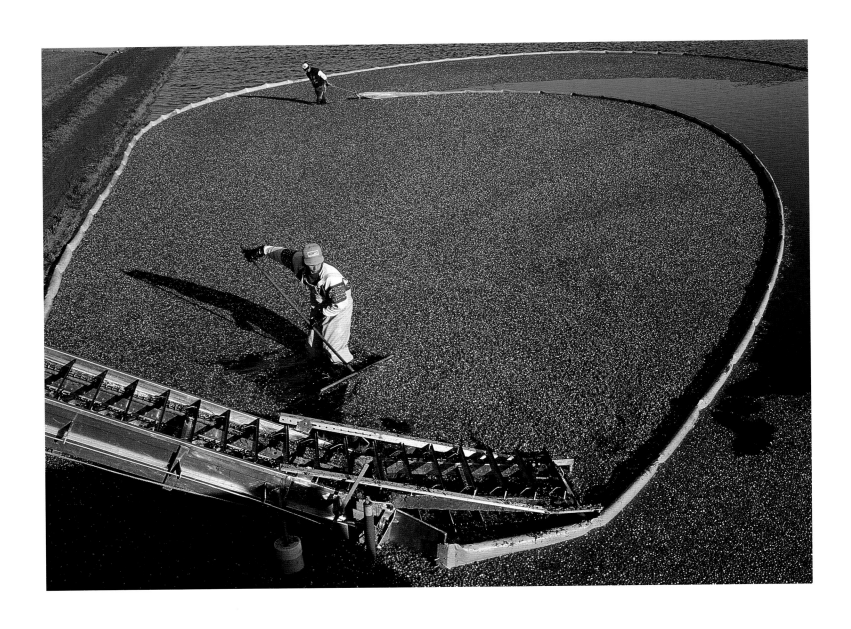

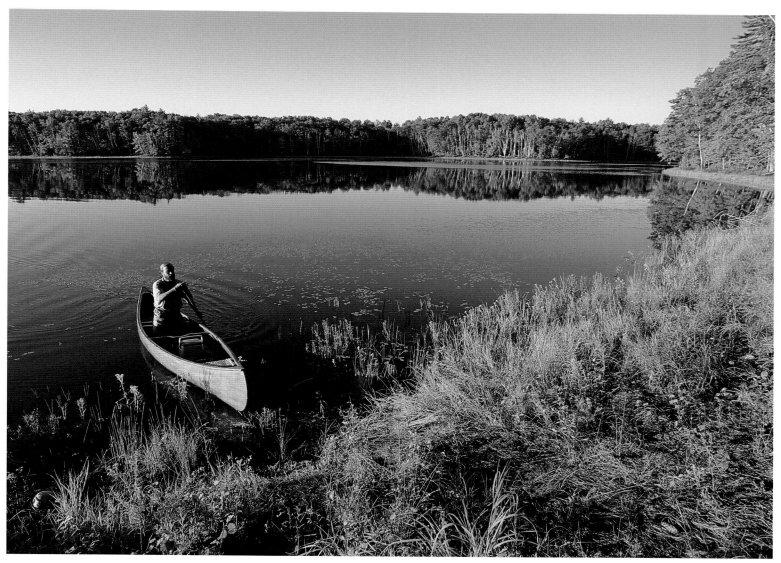

◄ Native to this country, the cranberry grows wild in acid bogs in many parts of the state. Commercial production is centered in Wood and Jackson counties. Cranberries are the state's largest fruit crop.
▲ The Land O'Lakes in northeastern Wisconsin is a region of big green woods and more than a thousand clear blue lakes. These lakes teem with bass, pike, muskellunge, and trout; provide habitat for a great variety of waterfowl; and attract a significant number of visitors from all over the nation to the state.

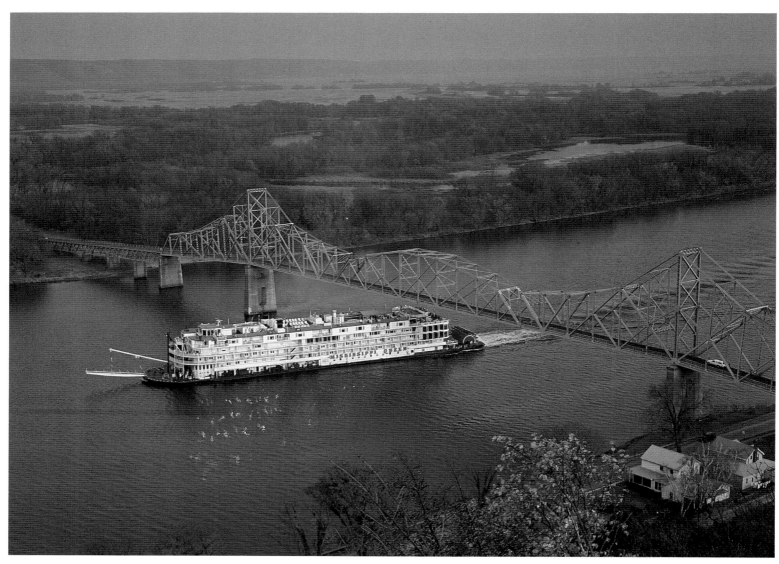

▲ Though the Mississippi days of Mark Twain are long past, the *Mississippi Queen* continues to run the Crawford County sloughs upriver from the juncture of the Wisconsin and Mississippi rivers, part of its round-trip journey between St. Paul and New Orleans.
▶ Door County is Wisconsin's "thumb," with 250 miles of shoreline jutting into Lake Michigan. Scenic vistas abound on both sides, drawing sightseers, water sports enthusiasts, and fishermen.

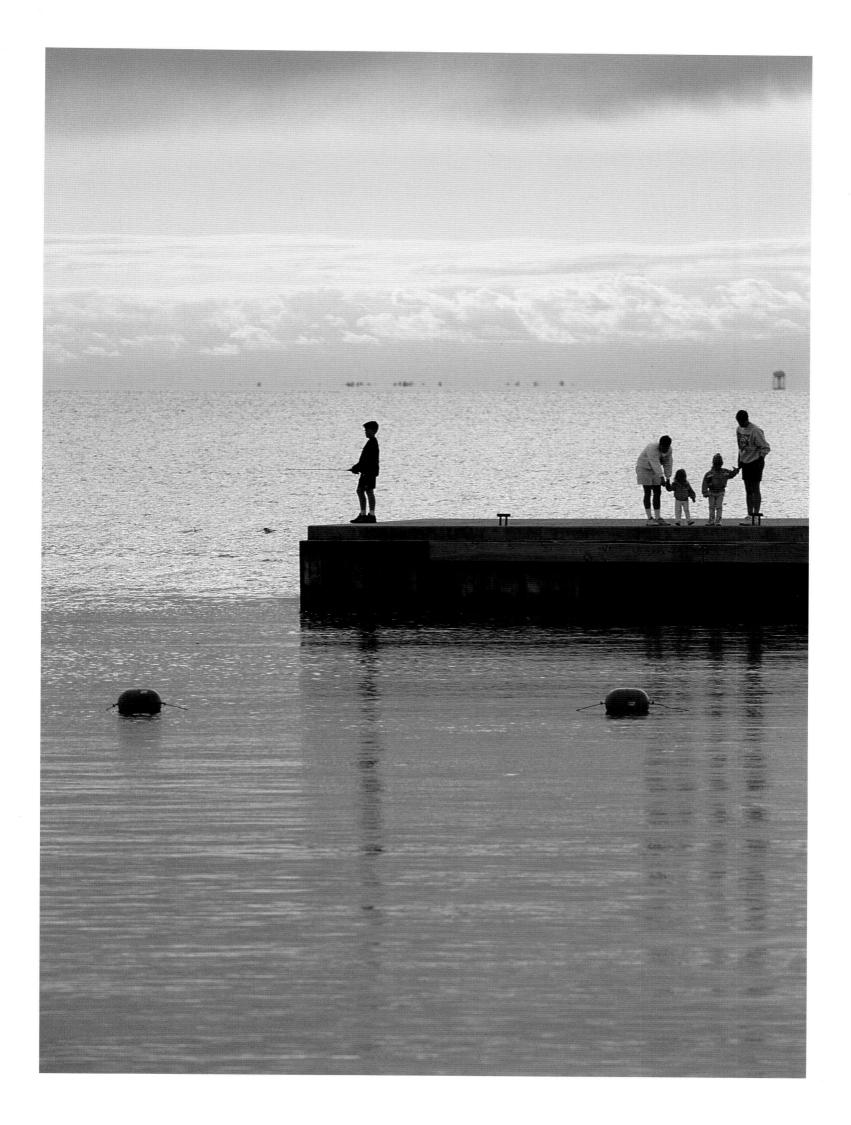

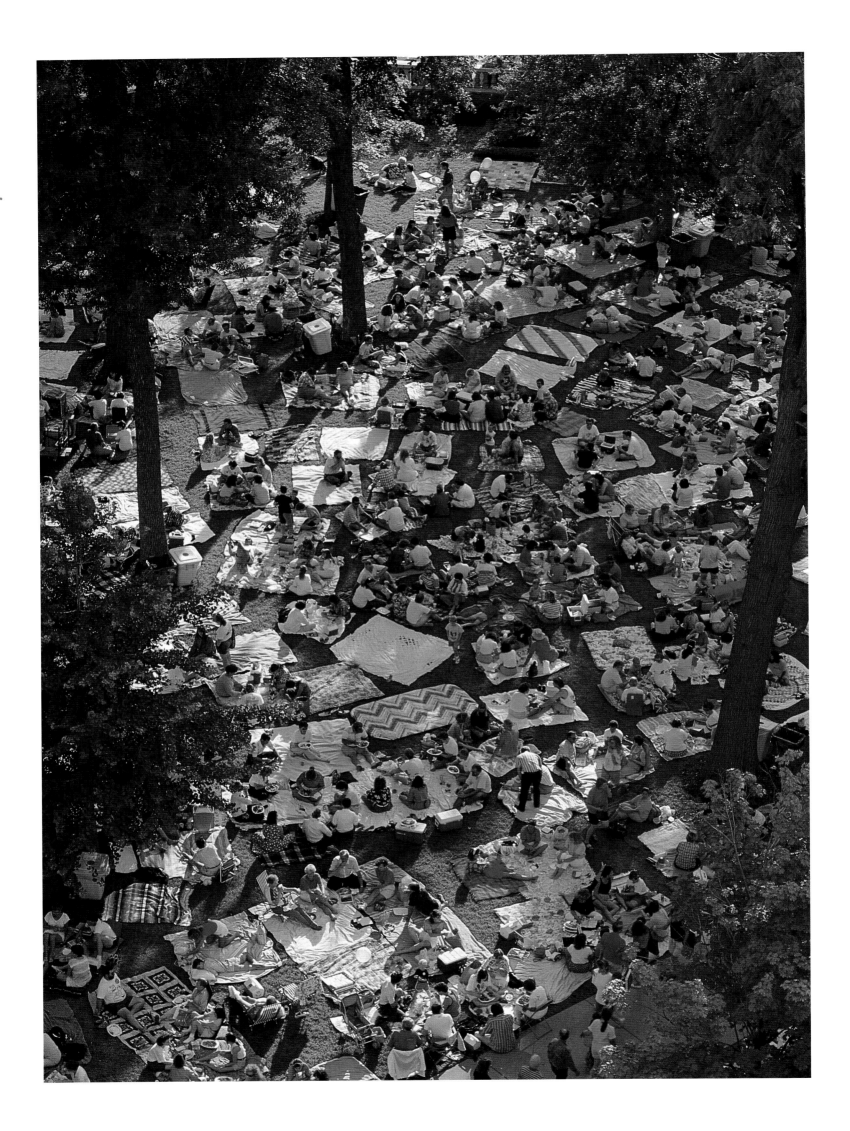

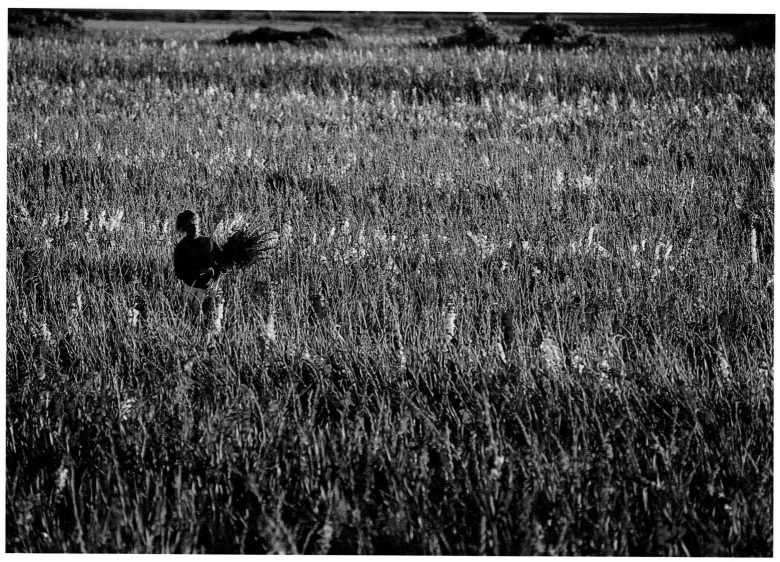

◄ "The Biggest Picnic of Summer" brings more than fifteen thousand to the Capitol Square on Wednesday evenings during the summer to hear the Wisconsin Chamber Orchestra. Now ten years old, the Concerts on the Square were conceived to bring people back to the downtown by featuring concert music programs in a festive picnic setting against the backdrop of the state Capitol.
▲ In the nearly level terrain of the Central Sands region between Lake Winnebago and the Wisconsin River is a soil ideal for the growth of vegetables and potatoes, and flowers such as gladiolus. Harvesting the bulbs in October is facilitated by the sandy soil.

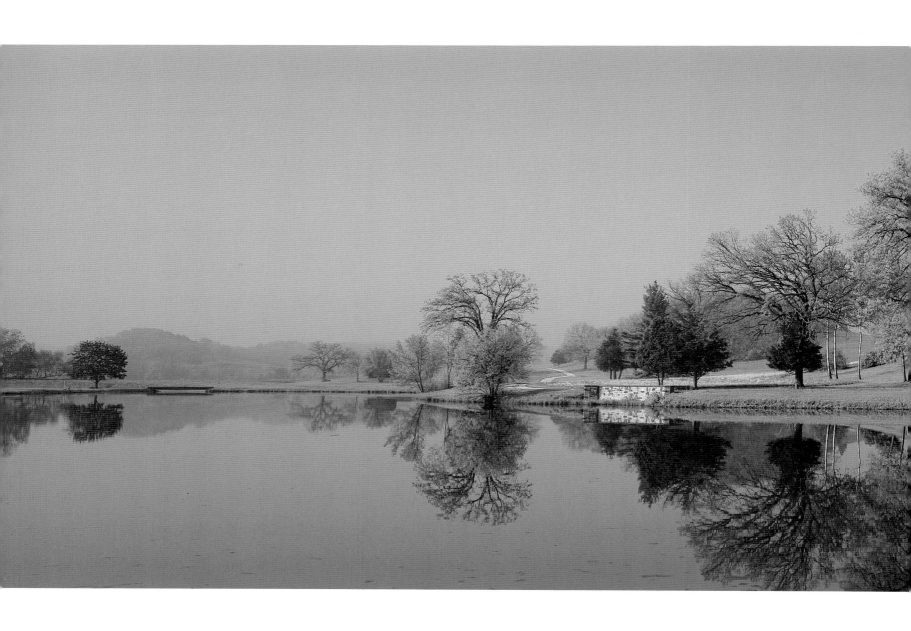

*The surfaces of Taliesin East induce serenity —
it is the mystery that Wright wanted to create.*

OWEN J. GROMME

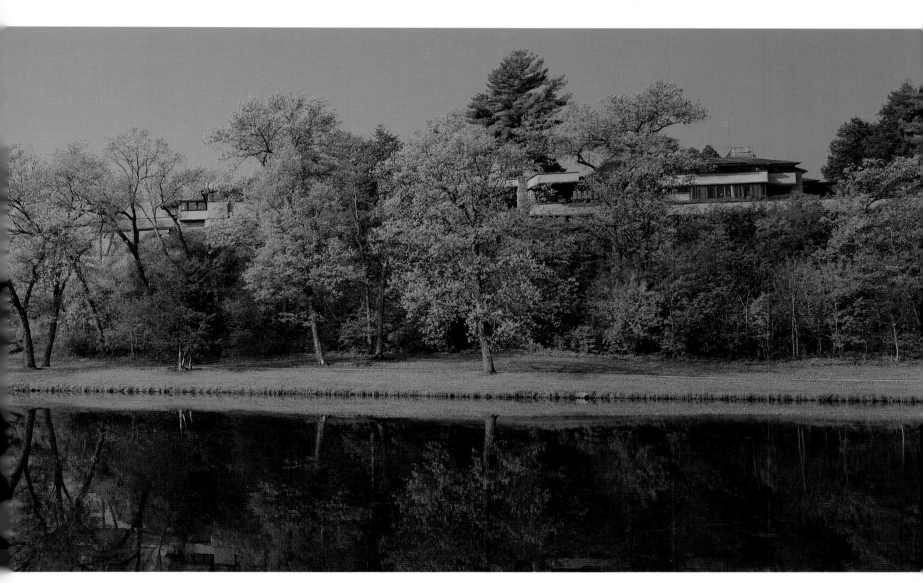

Frank Lloyd Wright's Taliesin East, Spring Green

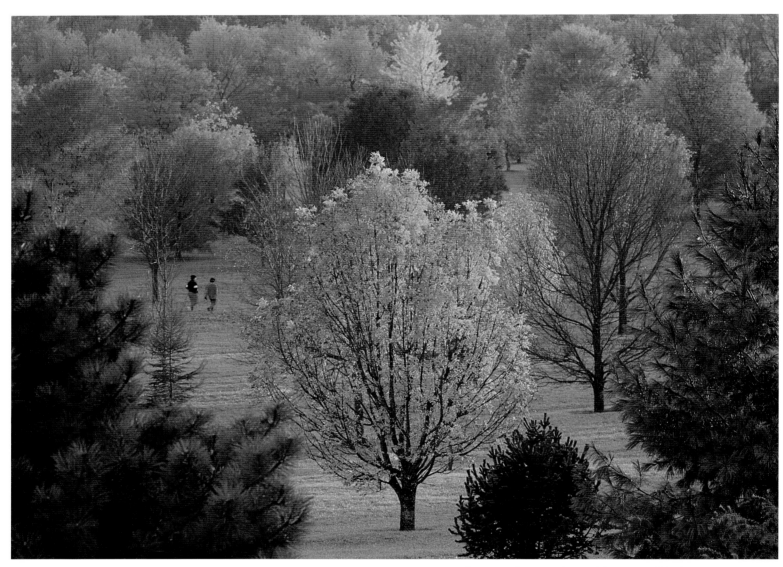

▲ Inspired by noted naturalist Aldo Leopold, the University of Wisconsin Arboretum is a 1,280-acre research and teaching laboratory that features restored biological communities including prairie, forest, and wetlands of the kind found in presettlement Wisconsin. Its Longenecker Gardens contain the largest woody plant collection in the state and is noted for its varieties of lilac and crabapple.
▶ The Flambeau River State Forest preserves one of Wisconsin's unspoiled wilderness areas. While roads now cut through the old timber, abundant wildlife hints of Wisconsin as it once was.

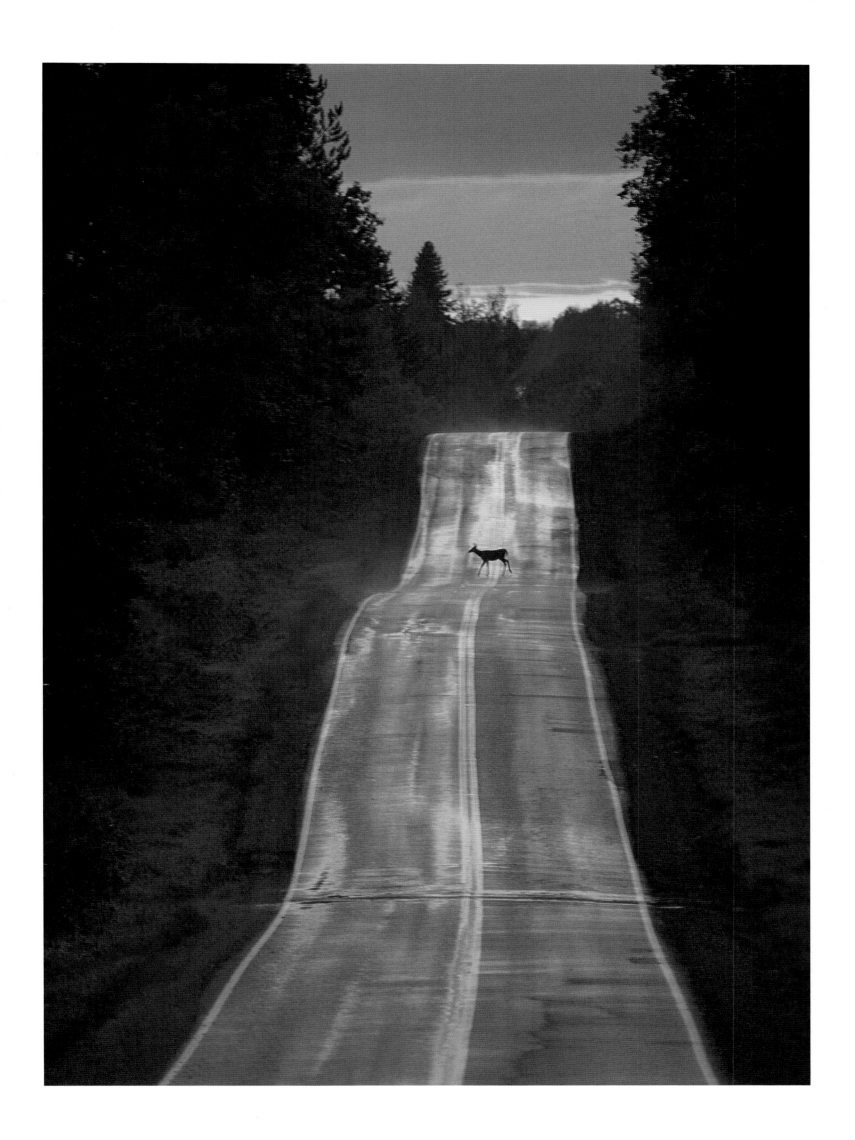

AFTERWORD

This is a book of contemporary photographs. Most of them were taken over a fifteen-month span. Many places, many subjects are not represented here. There are simply too many possibilities. I have aimed for a diversity of images that give a sense of place defined by land, people, culture, and imagination. There are photographs of yet unspoiled landscapes, appearing as they have for centuries; portraits of Wisconsinites working in much the same spirit as their ancestors; and images of the flights of fancy embodied in the fantastic folk-art and sculpture found around the state. For me, this has been a project of the heart. It has brought me back in touch with the land and people I grew up with. No matter how much I travel outside the state or country, I return *home* to Wisconsin.

The photographs in this book were taken with three different camera formats: 35mm Nikon, using 24mm to 400mm Nikon lenses; Pentax 67, with 45mm to 90mm lenses, and the Linhof 617 panoramic camera. Most photographs were taken on Fujichrome Velvia and 100 Professional film. The film was processed at Filmworks and Hyperion Studios in Madison, Wisconsin.

Thanks are due to many for the realization of this book. I owe a lot to very good teachers. One of the best was my first, Ruth Bernhard, who passed along an enduring sensitivity to the qualities of light. Thanks also go to Jay Maisel, who contributed to my appreciation of color photography at a crucial juncture. Peter Aaron, an architectural photographer, helped refine my sense of photographic construction and composition. And special appreciation goes to Sam Abell, whose sensibilities as a photographer and generosity as a teacher have enabled me to set high standards for my work.

Literally hundreds of Wisconsin citizens contributed in ways large and small to this project, from giving suggestions for picture ideas to pulling my car out of the snowbank. My mother, Ruth Williams Bennett, provided unflagging support and a "home away from home."

The officers and staff of the following agencies provided invaluable assistance: the State Historical Society of Wisconsin, the Department of Tourism and Development, the Wisconsin Nature Conservancy, the McKenzie Environmental Center, the Dane County Library System, the Department of Natural Resources, the University of Wisconsin, *Wisconsin Trails* magazine, and Third Coast Stock Source. Thanks also go to Larry Frankell and Fuji Film for their support and contribution; to Filmworks, Hyperion Studios, and Burne Color Lab—all of Madison—for their quality film processing and technical support.

I am indebted to my photo colleagues Brent Nicastro, Bob Rashid, Bruce Fritz, Greg Anderson, Dave Heberlein, and Woody Hagge for their advice and support. Special thanks to Mark E. Lefebvre for his assistance, editorial insights, and creation of a text that supports and complements the photographs. And it has been a pleasure to work with the staff at Graphic Arts Center Publishing Company, whose patience, willingness to listen to ideas, and attention to quality have helped to produce a wonderful book.

Most importantly, this book is dedicated to my wife, Mary, whose patience was limitless, companionship a joy, and sense of humor an absolute necessity. Like my best teachers, she has made me a better photographer and a better human being.

ZANE WILLIAMS